More Peanuts® Gang™ Collectibles

Jan Lindenberger &
Cher Porges

Schiffer® Publishing Ltd
4880 Lower Valley Road, Atglen, PA 19310 USA

Library of Congress Catalog Card Number: 98-88435

Designed by Bonnie M. Hensley
Type set in DomBold BT/Korinna BT

ISBN: 0-7643-0747-9
Printed in China
1 2 3 4

Published by Schiffer Publishing Ltd.
4880 Lower Valley Road Atglen, PA 19310
Phone: (610) 593-1777; Fax: (610) 593-2002
E-mail: Schifferbk@aol.com
Please visit our web site catalog at
www.schifferbooks.com

This book may be purchased from the publisher. Include $3.95 for shipping.
Please try your bookstore first.
We are interested in hearing from authors with book ideas on related subjects.
You may write for a free printed catalog.

In Europe, Schiffer books are distributed by Bushwood Books
6 Marksbury Avenue Kew Gardens
Surrey TW9 4JF England
Phone: 44 (0)181 392-8585; Fax: 44 (0)181 392-9876
E-mail: Bushwd@aol.com

Contents

Introduction

Welcome to book two of Peanuts collectibles. Of course, this doesn't represent every single collectible ever produced or available today. I am trying to give the collector an up-to-date general information and price guide for the Gang. There were and are so many wonderful pieces made that they would not even fit in two volumes!

In an age of everything but innocence, it's nice to know that some things are consistant. For nearly 50 years, the Peanuts Gang as represented a totally inoffensive world for us all to enjoy! Where else can you find dogs, birds, a round-headed kid, a kid with a security blanket, a loudmouthed girl in a booth, an African-American kid, a musician, humor and wit, all tied together with philosophical and theological overtones?

The creator of our favorite gang is Charles Monroe Schulz. In 1922, at the tender age of two days, Schulz was nicknamed Sparky by his uncle—after "Spark Plug", a horse featured in Barney Google comics. As Schulz was growing up in St. Paul, Minnesota, he would savor all the comics he could obtain, dreaming his own artwork would be published someday. After learning his craft through a mail-order art school, he began his career as a teacher for the same school. He went to New York in 1950 to seek publication of his comic strip "Li'l Folks" with United Features Syndicate. While the Syndicate liked Schulz's characters, they did not care for the name and soon changed it to *Peanuts*, a change Schulz was not fond of. Some editors of the Syndicate wanted to downplay the roll of Snoopy in the strip. Luckily Schulz gave him the prominent place he deserves in his work.

Charlie Brown, Patty, Shermy, and Snoopy had humble beginnings, in 7 newspapers. The Gang continued gaining popularity slowly, with subscribers coming and going. Only 18-20 newspapers subscribed in the first year. After some promotional planning, with small ads introducing the Peanuts Gang on an individual basis, growth finally occurred during the second year. At last, 1952 was time for the Sunday feature.

Also in 1952, John Selby, editor-in-chief at Rinehart & Company and a personal fan of the Peanuts, decided his favorite comic strip deserved a book. With the publication of *Peanuts* the book in 1952, the comic reprint business was off to a great start. With the exception of 1953, there has been a minimum of one book of reprinted Peanuts strips published per year. Not bad for this delightful comic!

What started out as a small group of four—Charlie Brown, Snoopy, and the all-but-forgotten Patty and Shermy—grew slowly into the cast of characters we all know and love. 1951 saw the introduction of Violet and Schroeder, who was soon playing Beethoven on a toy piano. Lucy and Linus Van Pelt arrived in 1952. Pig Pen began kicking up dirt in 1954. Sally Brown, Charlie Brown's sister, crawled into the strip in 1959. Patricia Reichardt, better known as Peppermint Patty, slid into home for the first time in 1966. Her best friend Marcie joined her in 1971. Birds resembling Woodstock had been flitting around since the late 1960s, and in 1970 Woodstock was officially named after the famous concert. Franklin, our African-American friend, came in 1968. The Van Pelt household had a new arrival in 1973 named Rerun. The Beagle Scouts, Woodstock's feathered colleagues, marched into the strip in the mid 1970s, and were eventually given individual names like Conrad, Oliver, and Bill in the late 1970s. Snoopy's first sibling from the Daisy Hill Puppy Farm—his brother Spike—was introduced in 1975. His sister Belle arrived next, in 1976. She was followed by her brother Marbles in 1982. Then came brother Olaf in 1989, and another brother, Andy, in 1994. Of course, this is not a complete list; with all of the characters coming and going it is impossible to list them all.

Now that we've established the arrival times of our favorite gang, let's discuss the evolution of these darling characters' personalities. In the beginning, the kids were almost interchangeable. Charles Schulz himself noted, "I was not sure who would become the hero or the heroine. I had trouble deciding because, at the time, Charlie Brown was not the put-upon character that he is now. Eventually I had trouble making Shermy anything but a straight man; Patty and a new girl, Violet, were serving merely as straight women; and Snoopy hadn't started thinking yet—so all the good lines were given to Charlie Brown."

Schroeder entering the scene as a baby changed that. It allowed the kids to interact with a baby, providing a good opportunity for jokes. His beginning to play the piano distinguished him even further. Linus and Lucy Van Pelt added family living to the scene. Brother-sister relations were shown as both fun and not-so-fun. Soon the characters invented their own opinions. Lucy got crabby; Snoopy began thinking up imaginary scenarios; Linus, toting a security blanket, got philosophical; and poor Charlie Brown got more depressed. Characters without much personality soon disappeared. The more notable newcomers were African-American Franklin, the Mexican-Swedish José Peterson, tomboy Peppermint Patty and her shadow Marcie.

Snoopy's character has changed immensley over the years.You can tell by his five different 2-dimensional copyright dates. When Snoopy first appeared in 1950, he always walked on 4 feet or sat on his haunches. This was his earliest copyright date. He earned another copyright in 1956 when he was shown dancing on two feet with his head high. By 1958 he was walking on two feet all the time, earning his third copyright date. His fourth copyright date came in 1965; his ears tucked under his aviator's hat and goggles covering his eyes, he began his battles as the Flying Ace against the Red Baron. His final copyright date came in1971, when Joe Cool appeared on the scene. Yet through all these changes he kept his loveable personality.

According to an April 1995 article by Jim Fleming for *Boomer* magazine, Mr. Schulz's comic strip has appeared in over 2,510 papers in 68 countries. By the late 1980s Peanuts was licensed to over 300 companies in 30 countries.

Over the years, countless items celebrating the Peanuts Gang have been treasured by collectors worldwide. Even though this second volume of Peanuts Gang collectibles still only scratches the surface of what's available, we hope it will give you a sampling of the vast range of Peanuts collectibles on the market.

With this history in mind, remember that the copyright date on the item does not reflect the year of manufacturing, only the year when the character on the piece was originally created. Thus, a piece with a 1965 copyright date may have been manufactured any year from 1965 through today.

Here are some hints on how to start collecting and where to find the Peanuts Gang:

The best place to buy, by far, is the Mid West Snoopy Swap Meet. This show and sale is put on by Laurel Sherry, who you can contact at 1723 Monroe St., New Holstein, Wisconsin, 53061. For information on the next meet, phone or fax 414-898-5578. Several hundred Snoopy fanatics get together to buy, sell, trade, and talk Snoopy. You will find not only Snoopy, but the rest of the Peanuts Gang in abundance. The prices are more than fair and the spirit amoung the sellers is very cheerful. For any Peanuts collector it's better than Christmas.

Searching for the Gang is fun and challenging. While waiting for the Snoopy swap meet, a good way to start a collection is to scour garage sales and flea markets. The prices are usually negotiable but the merchandise is not always mint. The more flaws, the less you should have to pay. Antique malls can also be fruitful. Prices are extremely variable, but depending on the condition and seller's knowledge, merchandise can be found at reasonable prices. If the item catches your eye and you *have* to have it, it's quite convenient to purchase it at the antique shop or mall. Remember the old slogan, "You snooze, you loose"? Purchase it when you see it or it may not be there when you go back. If you have more cash, toy shows are wonderful. Prices can be somewhat negotiable and merchandise is generally in good condition. There are also several toy magazines which list advertisements from all over the country. This is a good way to track down hard-to-find treasures.

For new items, a good source (especially around the holiday season when special things are available), is Knott's Berry Farms. Camp Snoopy usually has several selected new items.

Whatever path you choose to take in your search for Snoopy, remember the real search is for fun! I hope you enjoy this Peanuts Gang information and price guide.

Prices may vary according to area, availability and condition. Please take this guide with you on your search for Snoopy and Peanuts Gang, and happy hunting!

Acknowledgements

I wish to give a very special thank-you to Cher Porges and her family. Without Cher this Snoopy price guide would not have been possible. We worked many weeks and long hours to give this project the value it deserves. Her patience in arranging and rearranging her vast collection is greatly appreciated, and she even found things she had forgotten were there! The information for this price guide came from her years of knowledge and research. Between diet sodas, mustard pretzels, and my privilege of sleeping near "The Snoopy room", *Snoopy Collectibles*, books one and two, were born. With the large collection it turned out to be, we felt it warranted two books. Then it hit Cher that the Peanuts Gang needed their own two volumes. So be it. *Peanuts Gang Collectibles,* and now *More Peanuts Gang Collectibles*, have also been published. This meant longer hours, more days, and more diet soda. But the end result has been 4 much-needed all-color information and price guides. Mrs. Porges didn't mind the extra work—this gives everyone's Snoopy and Peanuts collections an up-to-date price guide. Thanks again, Cher, it was wonderful working with you; I have gained valuable friends in you and your family. That's the best part of this job. Thanks also to Laurel Sherry from New Holstein, Wisconsin—the show promotor for the Mid West Snoopy swap meet. Her patience was greatly appreciated for allowing me to photograph on showday as was her encouragement to do this book. Thanks to all the dealers at the show that let me photograph their Peanuts. For information about the Snoopy swap meet, contact Laurel by phone or fax at 414-898-5578.

Additional "Thank-you's" to:

Rose Elkins, St. Louis, Missouri

Warren Chamberlin, Mishawauka, Indiana.

Joel Martone, Colorado Springs, Colorado

Robert Meyer, St Louis, Missouri

Play it Again, Schroeder

Oh, Those Wonderful Music Boxes

Wooden music box, Snoopy playing hockey . Anri. Late 1960s. $75–100

Wooden music box, Snoopy ice skating. Anri. 1969. $80–100

Wooden music box, Charlie Brown at bat. Anri. Early 1960s. $75–100

Wooden music box, Lucy. Anri. Early 1970s. $140–160

Wooden music box, Lucy. Anri. 1969. $175–200

Wooden music box, Lucy and Snoopy. Anri. Early 1970s. $150–175

Wooden music box, Schroeder playing piano. Anri. Early 1970s. $150–175

Wooden music box, Snoopy the Flying Ace. Anri. Late 1960s. $75–100

Wooden music box, Lucy and Charlie Brown. Anri. 1969. $350–400

Wooden music box, Linus and Snoopy. Anri. Late 1960s. $75–100

Wooden music box, Linus and Snoopy. Anri. Early 1970s. $175–200

Wooden music box, Lucy and Charlie Brown under a mushroom umbrella. Anri. Early 1970s. $150–175

Wall-hanging wooden music box, Linus in Pumpkin Patch. 1971. Anri. $160–225

Ceramic music box, swinging Snoopy. Aviva. 1970s. $75–100

Jewelry box, Snoopy sitting on top of piano, wooden. Aviva. Mid 1970s. $60–80

Round plastic music box. Plays Swan Lake. 2 ¾" high. Aviva. 1982. $85–125

Wooden Peanuts Gang ferris wheel bank. Insert coin in back to activate musical action. Early 1970s. Schmid. $200–250

Wooden music box, Red Baron in airplane—the Flying Ace's nemesis. Schmid. Early 1970s. $200–300

Wooden music box, Flying Ace Snoopy in airplane. Schmid. Early 1970s. $250–350

Ceramic musical cup, Charlie Brown. Schmid. Early 1970s. $50–75

Ceramic musical cups, Charlie Brown and Lucy. Schmid. 1971. Charlie Brown $60–80. Lucy $50–70.

Ceramic Linus musical bank. Also available: Snoopy and Charlie Brown. Put in coin and music is activated. Schmid. $75–120

Ceramic Peanut Gang music box. Schmid. Limited edition. Mid 1980s. $85–125

Ceramic music box, Lucy. Schmid. Mid 1980s. $75–100

Ceramic Christmas music box, Charlie Brown, Lucy and Snoopy. Schmid. 1986. $100–125

Ceramic music box, Schroeder and Snoopy. Schmid. 1983. First limited edition. $80–110

Ceramic music box, Charlie Brown. Schmid. Mid 1980s. $75–100

Ceramic music box, Snoopy in a gift box. Snoopy goes up and down. Schmid. Mid 1980s. $75–100

Ceramic music box, Charlie Brown and Snoopy. Schmid. 1980. $100–125

Charlie Brown music box. Schmid. Mid-1970s. $100–125.

Ceramic Christmas music box, Lucy. Schmid. Mid 1980s. $75–100

Ceramic music box, twirling Snoopy, Belle and Woodstock. Schmid. Mid 1980s. $85–125

Ceramic music box, Charlie Brown. Schmid. Mid 1980s. $60–80

Ceramic music boxes—Charlie Brown, Snoopy and Lucy. Schmid. Mid 1980s. 5" x 6" $75–100. 12" $200–250

Ceramic music box. Woodstocks move up and down to "Let it Snow, Let it Snow." 8½" x 5". Willits. Late 1980s. $150–175

Ceramic music box, Lucy and Charlie Brown ice skating. Willitts. Late 1980s. $40–60

Ceramic music box, Lucy. Willitts. 1990. $40–60

Porcelain music box, 40th anniversary cake with whole Peanuts Gang. Willitts. 1990. $150–250

Snoopy carousel music box. Willitts. 1989–90. $50–75

Ceramic automobile music boxes. The entire gang in auto is most valuable. Willitts. Late 1980s. $125–200

Ceramic music box, Charlie Brown on sofa with Snoopy and Woodstock. 1990. Willitts. $40–60

Carousel music box. Willitts. Late 1980s. $150– 200

Ceramic music box, Schroeder and Lucy. Willitts. Late 1980s–90s. $40–60

Plastic music box, Santa Snoopy with globe and toys. 1990. The last Willitts music box. (The train rotates around the world.) $40–60

Ceramic music box, Sally carrying Snoopy. Willitts. 1990. $40–60

Ceramic music boxes. Sally, Charlie Brown, Lucy. 4". Japan. 1990s. $50–60 each.

Plastic music box. Willitts. Late 1980s. $30–40

Sound of Peanuts

A Boy Named Charlie Brown and *Oh Good Grief* CDs.1980s. $15–20 each.

Record, *A Boy Named Charlie Brown*. 1970. $15–20

Record, *You're a Good Man, Charlie Brown*. 1973. $15–20

Record, *Charlie Brown's All-Stars*, late1970s. $15–20

Record, *It's the Great Pumpkin, Charlie Brown*. 45 RPM. 1978. $7–11

Record, *It was a Short Summer, Charlie Brown*. 45 RPM. 1980. $7–11

Tape, *It's About Love, Charlie Brown*. Venture. 1994. $6–9

Record, *You're in Love, Charlie Brown*. 45 RPM. 1978. $7–11

Music books, *Snoopy's favorite Piano Solos* and *Schroeder's First Recital*. Published by Studio 224, which was later renamed Houston Publishing. 1980 – 1990s. $6–12 each.

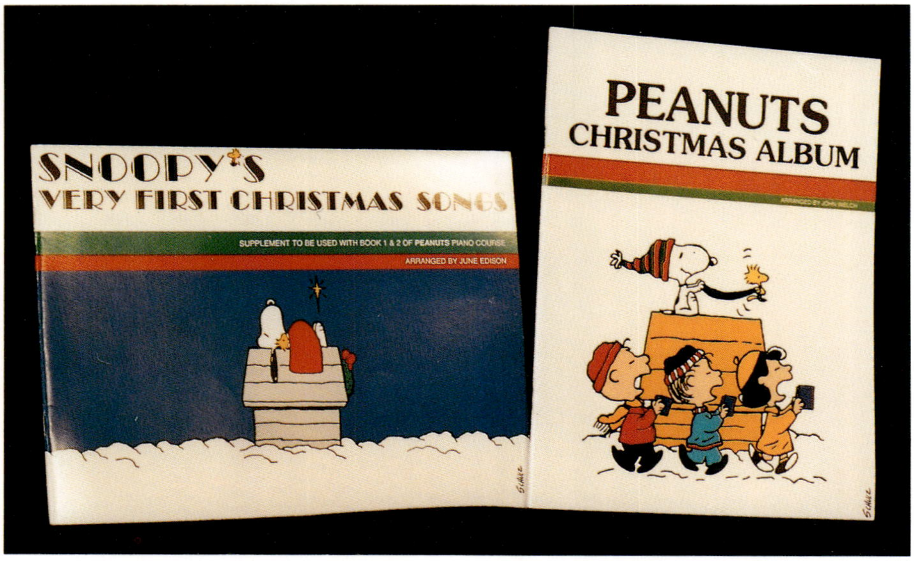

Music books, *Snoopy's Very First Christmas Songs* and *Peanuts Christmas Album*. Published by Studio 224, which was later renamed Houston Publishing. 1980–1990s. $6–12 each.

Piano music from Houston Publishing. 1980–1990s. $6–12 each.

Plastic radio, Snoopy, Woodstock, and Charlie Brown. 2-dimensional image. Concept 2000/ Mattel Co. Late 1970s. $35–50

Plastic Snoopy radio. Determined. 1977. 7 ½" x 8". $75–100

Holiday Fare

It's Great Pumpkin Time, Linus

Nylon screen-printed flag, Linus and the Great Pumpkin. New Creative Enterprises, Inc. Mid 1990s. $10–15

Wooden Halloween outdoor decoration. NCE. 1996. $15–20

The Peanuts Book of Pumpkin Carols. Hallmark. 1970s. This booklet has been reissued and is currently available. $4–8

The Peanuts Book of Pumpkin Carols. Hallmark. Another variation of this book. $4–8

Plastic Snoopy pumpkin cutter. Metal. Late 1980s. $6–9

Super Bubble treat bucket. Bucket held 125 pieces of bubble gum. Mid 1990s. $3–5

Rubber Charlie Brown mask. Topstone. Mid 1990s. $15–20

Halloween Peanuts Gang PVC figurines. Applause. 1990. $4–7 each.

Cardboard Halloween candy boxes from Whitman's. Mid 1990s. $2–3 each.

Rubber Pigpen and Lucy masks from Topstone. 1990s. $15–20 each.

Charlie Brown costume and mask, vinyl. 1980s. Collegeville Costumes. $20–25 mint, in box.

Hearts to you, Lucy

Peanuts Gang chocolate candy by Whitman's. 1996. $4–6

Plastic purse with box of chocolates inside from Whitman's. First available Valentine's day. 1997. $5–7

Easter Beagle comes to town

Keepsake ornament from Hallmark. First in a series of 3. 1994. $15–20

Easter puzzle greeting. Hallmark. 1980s. $5–7

Easter figures of Lucy and Linus. PVC fun figures. Applause. 1990. $5–7 each.

Jingle all the way, Sally

A Charlie Brown Christmas, 1995—30th Anniversary of the Christmas television special. A Hallmark special promotion, they were not available until after Thanksgiving, when two characters were released. One week later the other characters were released. Within about a week of that, they sold out everywhere! They were priced so reasonably even non-collectors bought them. This store display has a lucite cover. Just the characters and base in boxes, \$50–75. Display cards, cover, snow bank, set of figures in boxes, \$125–175.

Ceramic Christmas ornament. Snoopy dressed as Santa. Determined. 1980. 3". \$40–50

Ceramic Christmas wreath. Determined. 6 ½". Early 1980s. \$150–175. Not shown: same figure, larger size. \$175–200

Ceramic candle holder. Holds large candle. 3" x 4". Willitts. Early 1990s. $40–50

Ceramic Christmas planter. Determined. Mid 1970s. 7 ½". $75–90

Ceramic Chrismas planters. Determined. Mid 1970s. $60–75 each.

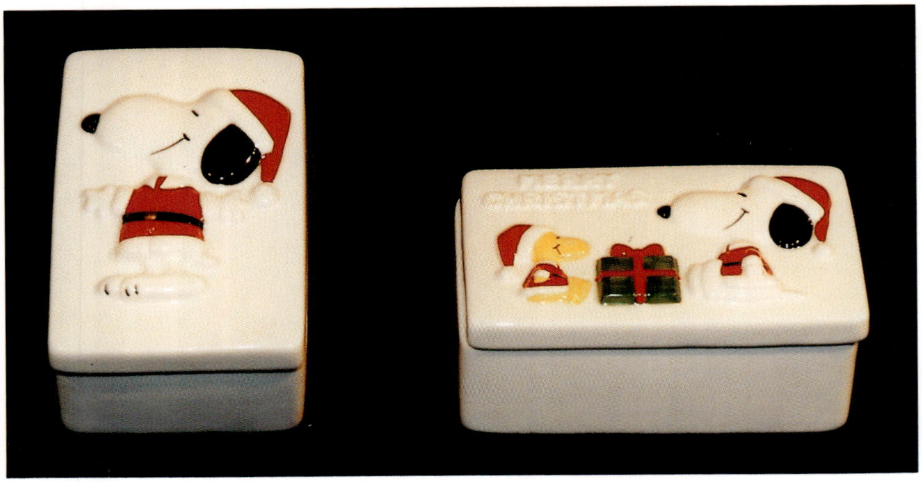

Ceramic Christmas boxes, raised pictures and lettering. 4 ½" x 2 ¾" x 2". Determined. Late 1970s. $50–60 each.

Ceramic Christmas steins. Left to right: "Merry Christmas 1975" on back. "Merry Christmas 1976" on back. "Merry Christmas 1977" on back. Determined. 3 ¾". $30–40 each.

Ceramic Christmas steins. Left to right. "Merry Christmas 1978" on back. "Merry Christmas 1979" on back. "Merry Christmas 1980" on back. Determined. 3 ¾". $30–40 each.

Ceramic Christmas steins. Left to right. "Merry Christmas 1981" on back. "Merry Christmas 1982" on back. 3 ¾". $30–40 each. Not shown: Santa Snoopy stuffing toys into his sack, seven Woodstocks helping with toy making and wrapping, "Merry Christmas 1983" on back. Determined. $30–40

Tin Christmas set. Tray, candle, coasters, etc. Tray, $25–35, accessories $15–20 each.

Hallmark Panorama Balls. Before 1979 Hallmark only offered glass and satin ball ornaments. Then in 1979 came a plastic 3-D ball with the most totally cool Snoopy scene in it; the most innovative *Peanuts* ornament ever made. They were inexpensive at first, but became more expensive year by year—worth saving up for! In 1979 the price was $8.00; by 1983 they were selling for $13.00 each. After 1979 the balls were never on the shelves long enough to be discounted at half price, which is Hallmark's usual answer to leftover merchandise when the season passes. The first 1979 ball is not pictured here in the correct box. The original box was a 5" x 5" gold box with blue lining and clear plastic lid. The remainder of the boxes are as shown with a matching lid (same as the base) and a clear plastic cover in between. Finding these balls without the box in mint condition or in the box mint condition is hard to do as they sometimes yellowed in the box.

Hallmark panorama ball Christmas ornament. "Ski Holiday." 1980. (2nd in a series of 5) $100–125

Hallmark panorama ball Christmas ornament. "Ice Hockey Holiday." 1975. (1st of a series of 5) 1979. $150–175

Hallmark panorama ball Christmas ornament. "Snoopy and Friends" (3rd in a series of 5). $100–125.

The first few years of a wonderful collaboration are most memorable: Christmas, plus Hallmark, plus Peanuts. The boxes for 1977 and 1978 ornaments were little red dog houses. The first 2 years of the Hallmark series were glass and satin balls exclusively. Balls continued onward with the addition of wonderful other types of ornaments. 1977's series included a double glass set (pictured), a dated satin (pictured), and a glass ornament with Schroeder, his piano, and Lucy(pictured). 1978 featured satin only, with Charlie Brown wrapped in Christmas lights (pictured), Joy to the World—Peanuts Gang Caroling(pictured), Snoopy/Woodstock taking a fresh cut tree to decorate, and Santa Snoopy hanging filled stockings. 1979 featured the panorama ball, the Grandson satin ball, and a satin ball entitled "Time to Trim." 1980 featured the panorama ball and one satin ball.

Hallmark panorama ball Christmas ornament. Snoopy and Friends. 1982. (4th in a series of 5) $100–125

Satin Christmas ornament in box. Hallmark. First year: 1977. $50–70 mint, in box. $70–85 mint.

Hallmark panorama ball Christmas ornament. Santa Snoopy. 1983. (5th in a series of 5) $100–125

Satin Christmas ornament in box. Hallmark. Second year: 1978. $50–70 mint, in box.

Satin Christmas ornament in box. Hallmark. Second year: 1978. $50–70 mint, in box.

Glass Christmas ornament. Hallmark. 1977. First year. $50–70 mint, in box.

Glass Christmas ornament set in box. Hallmark. First year. 1977. $80–100 mint, in box.

Christmas ornament, Snoopy hugging Woodstock. Hallmark. 1990. $30–40 mint, in box.

Christmas ornament, Snoopy skiing. Hallmark. 1984. $80–95.

Christmas ornament, Linus on sled. Hallmark. 1995. $25–40 mint, in box.

Ornament, Lucy with football. Hallmark. 1995. $10–15 each.

Plastic Peanuts Gang ornaments. These ornaments came as shown (poorly painted) 1980s. $2–3 each.

Ornament, Woodstock pulling a sled with a tree on top. Hallmark, first miniature Peanuts ornament. 1996. $20–30 mint, in box.

Musical Christmas ornament, Schroeder and Lucy. Hallmark. 1996. $30–45 mint, in box.

Peanuts Gang Christmas ornaments. Hallmark. Left: This personalized ornament was offered in 1995, specially made with your own words. Right: glass ball, 1993. $15–20 each.

Christmas ornament, Snoopy, flickering light. Hallmark. Magic collector series, first year. 1991. $60–80 mint, in box.

Christmas ornament, Snoopy and Woodstock, flickering light. Hallmark Magic collector series. 1994. $50–60 mint, in box.

Plastic Christmas ornament, light and motion. Hallmark. 1995. (5th in the Peanut series) $60–75 mint, in box.

Goldtone Peppermint Patty heart-shaped ornament. 1980s. $10–15

Wooden Christmas ornaments. Determined. 1980s. $7–10 in package.

Ceramic ornaments, Snoopy Bicentennial series. Determined. 1976. $35–40 each.

Ceramic ornaments, Western series. Determined. 1981. $35–40 each.

Ceramic ornaments, International series. Determined. 1977. $35–50

Ornaments, Adventure series, ceramic. Determined. 1975. $35–40 each.

Ceramic ornaments, International series. Determined. 1977. $35–40 each.

Ceramic ornaments, Musical series. Determined. 1976. $35–40 each.

Ornaments, Sport series, ceramic. Determined. 1975–76. $35–40 each.

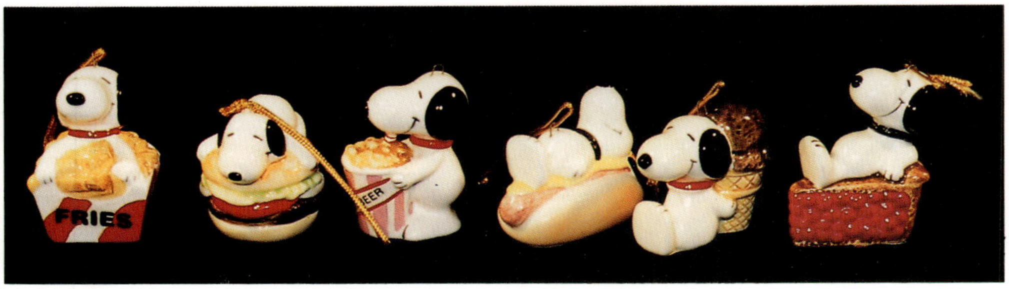

Ceramic ornaments, Junk food series. Determined. 1981–82. $35–40 each.

Ceramic ornaments. Determined. 1980–81. $35–40 each.

Ceramic ornaments, Transportation series. Determined. 1979. $35–40 each.

Ceramic ornament, Snoopy with surf board. Determined. 1970s. $35–40

Ceramic ornaments, Red Santa cap series. Determined. 1979–80. $35–40 each.

Ceramic ornaments. Determined. 1980. $35–40 each.

Ceramic Christmas ornaments. Determined. 1977. $35–40 each.

Ceramic Christmas ornaments. Determined. 1981. $35–40 each.

Ceramic Christmas ornaments. Determined. 1972–75. $35–40 each.

Ceramic Christmas ornaments. Determined. 1979. $35–45 each. Not shown: Sitting Snoopy with candy cane with "Merry Christmas 1979" across cap fur. Snoopy sleeping on doghouse with "Merry Christmas 1979" on back wall. Snoopy reclining atop large wreath with red bone with "Merry Christmas 1979" on back. $35–40 each.

Ceramic Christmas ornaments. Determined. 1978. $35–40 each.

Ceramic Christmas ornaments. Determined. 1982. $35–40 each.

Ceramic Christmas Cable car series, ornaments. Determined. 1970s. $35–40 each. Not pictured: Woodstock wearing Santa cap and sitting on green cable car.

Ceramic Christmas ornaments. Determined. 1975. $35–40 each.

Ceramic Christmas ornaments. Flat series. Determined. 1978. $35–40 each.

Ceramic Christmas ornaments. Determined. 1980. $35–40 each.

Ceramic Christmas ornaments. Musician series. Determined, 1976. $35–40 each.

Peanuts Gang ornaments, plastic resin. Danbury Mint. Bought individually only through Danbury Mint. Storage box included when all were purchased. 1990s. $15–20 each or $250–350 set with box.

Peanuts Gang ornaments, plastic resin. Danbury Mint. Bought individually only through Danbury Mint. Storage box included when all were purchased. 1990s. $15–20 each or $250–350 set with box.

Front and back of china Christmas bell ornaments. Determined. 1980s. $25–35 each.

Front and back of china Christmas bell ornaments. Determined. 1980s. $25–35 each.

Ceramic Christmas ornaments. Willits. Late 1980s–early 1990s. $30–35 each

Ceramic Christmas ornaments. Willitts. Late 1980s or early 1990s. $30–35 each.

Plastic Carousel ornament by Willitts. Turn top of carousel and characters go up and down. Late 1980s. $50–60

Peanuts Signature Collection Ornaments. Porcelain disk ornaments. Willitts. 1990. $20–25 in box.

Felt Christmas ornamentsmade from kit. Malina. Late 1970s. $10–15 each.

Plastic Lucy ornament. Came in a kit, with paint. Available in all characters. Late 1970s. $2–3 each or $25–35 complete set.

Plastic Charlie Brown ornament. (Also included in set with Lucy). Came in a kit, with paint. Available in all characters. Late 1970s. $2–3 each or $25–35 complete set.

Glass Polonnaise Christmas ornaments. Kurt S. Adler Co. 1997. If bought as a set, they came in a wooden box suitable for display. $130–150. If bought individually, a cardboard box, $35–45 each.

Resin Christmas ornaments. Kurt S. Adler Co. 1997. $4–6 each.

Stuffed plush Christmas ornaments. Kurt S. Adler Co. 1997. $7–10 each.

Wooden Christmas ornaments in packages. Kurt S. Adler Co. 1997. $3–7 each.

Wooden Christmas ornaments in packages. Kurt S. Adler Co. 1997. $3–7 each.

Wooden Christmas ornaments in packages. Kurt S. Adler Co. 1997. $3–7 each.

Plastic Snoopy string of lights. Kurt S. Adler Co. 1997. $20–30 with box.

Christmas ornaments from Silvestri. Early 1990s. $15–25 set.

Mini package toppers, cotton. Applause. 1990. $10–12 each.

Resin ornaments on display board. Silvestri. Early 1990s. $12–15 each. $90–125 as shown.

Resin ornaments, Peanuts Gang in stockings. Silvestri. Production was short lived, 2–3 years. Early 1990s. Individually $12–15 each. $65–75 set.

Resin ornaments, Peanuts Gang skating. Silvestri. Early 1990s. $12–15 each. $65–75 set.

Christmas ornaments from Silvestri. Early 1990s. $35–40 set.

Christmas ornaments from Silvestri. Early 1990s. $12–15 set.

Cotton Christmas ornaments in original store display box. Dakin. 1996. $6–10 each. Box $5–7

Cotton stuffed Christmas wreath. Cut and stuff. FCI. Early 1980s. $15–20

Cotton Peanuts Gang Christmas stocking. Determined. 1980s. $15–20

Cotton Peanuts Gang Christmas stocking. Determined. 1980s. $15–20

Plastic Christmas tree skirt with felt back. 1980s. $8–12

Charlie Brown cookie tin. Mid 1990s. Sonoma Valley Foods. Contained chocolate chip cookies. $5–8

Christmas Snoopy Santa and Sleigh Set for outdoors. Intex. Late 1980s. $40–50

Tin popcorn container. 1990s. $10–15

Peanuts box of candy. Whitman's. 1995. $1–2

Bank, plastic Snoopy on Christmas dog house. Whitman's. Mid 1990s. Filled with candy. $4–6

Plush Woodstock angel tree topper. Handmade from licensed toy. 1980s. $20–30

Plush Snoopy angel tree topper. Handmade from a licensed toy. 1980s. $20–30

When You Care Enough to Send the Very Best

Hallmark & Ambassador

Boxed cards, Snoopy's brother Spike. "It's beginning to look a lot like Christmas." Hallmark. Early 90s. $15–20

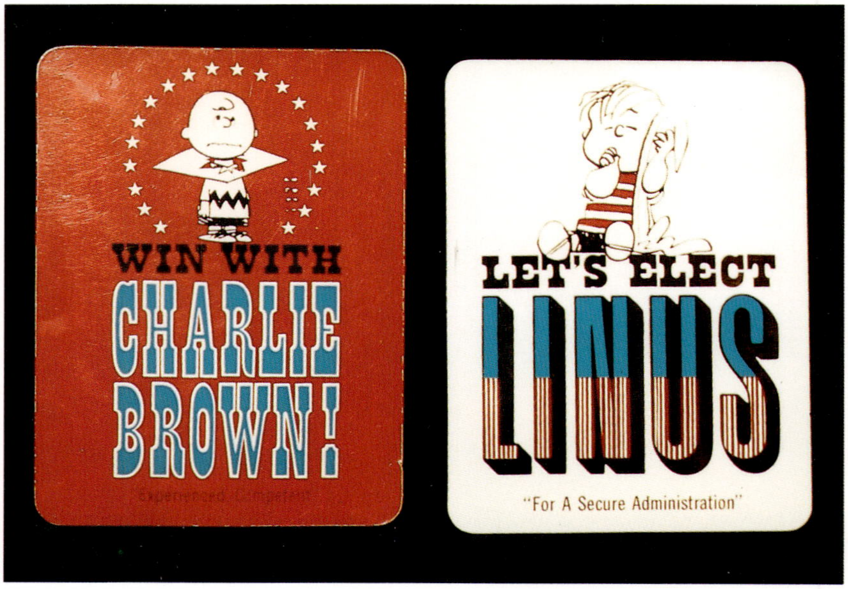

Charlie Brown and Linus cards. Hallmark, 1970s. $10–20 each.

Book, *The Peanuts Platform*. 1970s. $15–25

Paper centerpiece, Schroeder, Snoopy, and Woodstock. Ambassador. 1980s. $12–18

Paper centerpiece, Carnival Capers. Hallmark. 1980s. $12–18

Centerpiece, Great Pumpkin. 12 ½". Hallmark. Early 1970s–80s. $15–20

Centerpiece, Happy Birthday. Hallmark. Late 1980s. $10–15

Card Holder, Peanuts Express. Hallmark. 1970s. $15–20

Centerpiece, Snoopy. Hallmark. 1970s. $15–20

Picture, Christmas is for Sharing. Hallmark. Early 1980s. $10–15

Centerpiece, Peanuts Rainbow Party. 10 ¼". Hallmark. 1970s. $15–20

Centerpiece, Peanuts Rainbow Party. 10 ¼". Hallmark. Late 1980s. $10–15

Hallmark plaquettes. Early 1970s. Approx 3" x 4". $10–12 each.

Plastic covered cards. Snoopy design on plastic, wrapped over plain card. Approximately 3 x 5". Late 70s. $4–8 each.

Card. Hallmark, 1980s. $3–6

Etichette Peanuts (French). Hallmark. $8–15

Scrap book. Each page has black, white, and red pictures of gang. Early 1970s. $35–45

Snoopy's Daily Dozen—Exercise With the Entire Gang! Late 1960s, early 1970s. Hallmark. $25–35

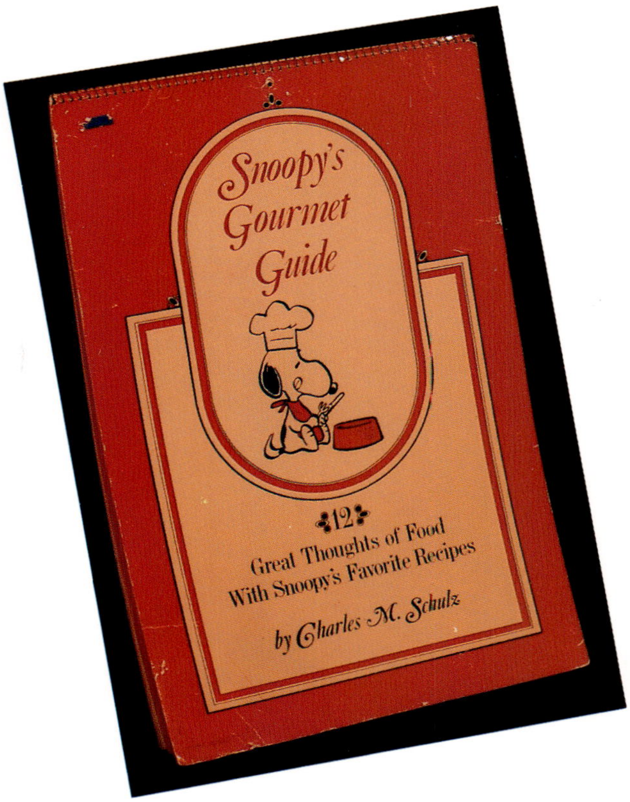

Hallmark Gourmet Guide. (With inside page shown also) 1960s–70s. $25–30

Sticker coloring poster, with stickers. Ambassador. 1980s. $5–7

Cocktail Napkins. Hallmark. Early 1970s. $12–18 complete set in box.

Cocktail Napkins. Hallmark. Early 1970s. $12–18 complete set in box.

Flying Ace paper napkins. Battle Ready and Battle Worn. Hallmark. Late 1970s. $8–10 complete in package.

Snoopy Napkins. Hallmark. 1980s. $5–7

Greeting card with holder pouch. Shows fold-out. Hallmark. Late 1960s. $15–20 set.

Greeting cards, boxed. Hallmark. Late 1960s. $15–20 set.

Package of greeting cards from Hallmark. Early 1970s. $15–20 complete set.

Christmas greeting cards. Hallmark. 1970s. $2–3 each.

Christmas stand–up greeting cards. Hallmark. Early 1970s. $12–15

Snoopy note card. Part of Peanuts Friend-to-Friend Cards. Individually $1–2

Peanuts Friend-to-Friend Cards. Top of tablet of cards. Complete. 1980s. $15–20 mint.

Greeting cards from Hallmark. Early 1970s. $5–9 each.

Peanuts postage stickers booklet. Hallmark printed these in other languages. 1980s. $10–15

Party invitations from Hallmark. Late 1960s–early 1970s. $7–9

Charlie Brown, cardboard on stick. Ambassador. Early 1990s. $4–6

Cardboard stick sign, Sally. Hallmark. 1980s. $4–6

13 press-out decorations. Hallmark. 1980s. $10–12

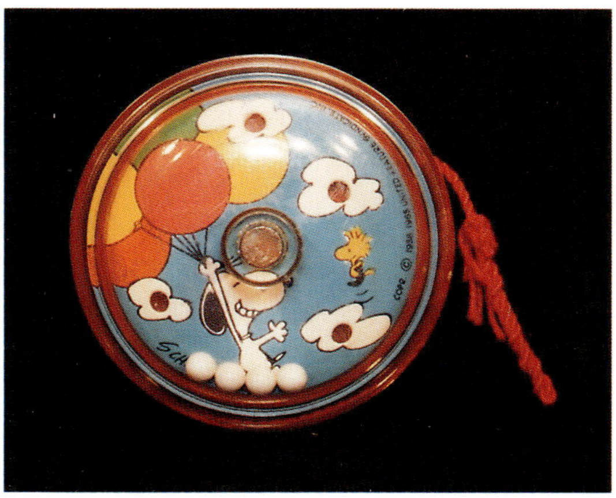

Snoopy yo-yo, plastic. Hallmark, 1980s. $7–20 mint on card.

Goodnight, Charlie Brown

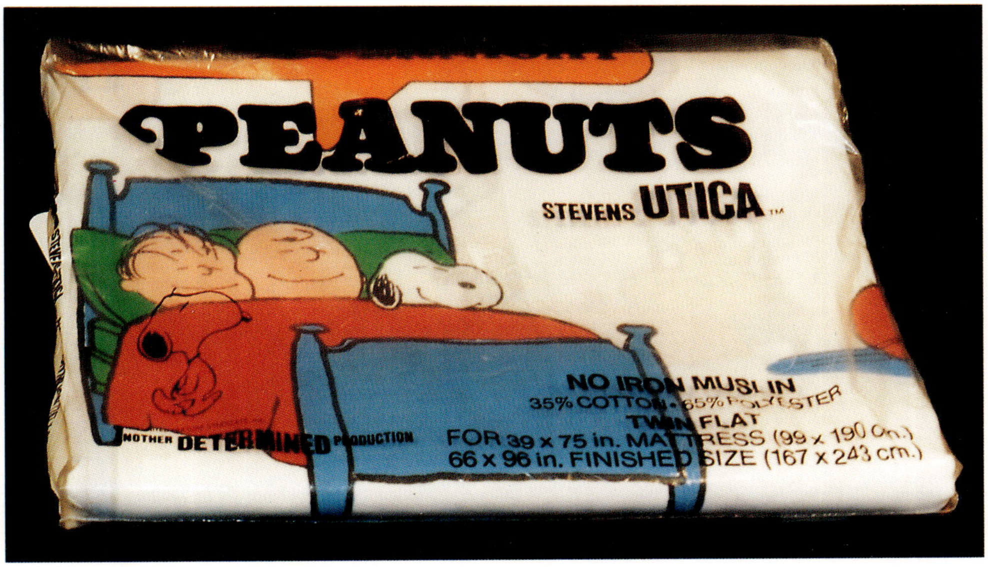

Twin-size sheet, muslin. Determined. Utica. Stevens. 1980s. $12–15

Peanuts Gang full-size sheet, cotton. 1980s. Utica. $15–20

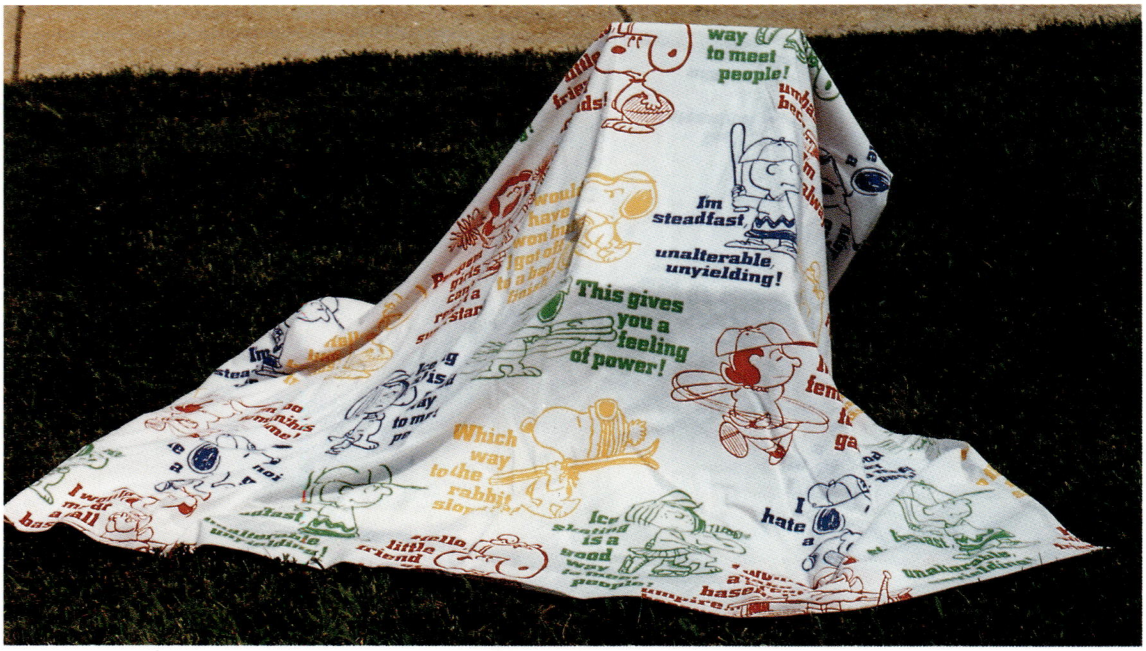

Cotton sheet, Peanuts Gang. Tastemaster by J.P. Stevens & Co., Inc. 1980s. Twin $10–15; full $20–25 mint, in package.

Cotton sheet, Peanuts Gang. Tastemaster by J.P. Stevens & Co., Inc. Late 1970s–early 1980s. Twin sheet $10–15; full $20–25 mint.

Cotton sheet, Peanuts Gang. Tastemaster by J.P. Stevens & Co., Inc. Mid to late 1970s. Twin $10–15; full $20–25 mint, in package.

Cotton pillow case, Peanuts Gang, castle. Opposite side of Western Gang.

Cotton pillow case. Tastemaster by J.P. Stevens & Co., Inc. Probably late 1970searly 1980s. $5–7 mint in package.

Cotton pillow case with Western Peanuts Gang. J.P Stevens Taste maker. Early 1980s. $5–7 mint pkg.

Acrylic blanket. Chatham. This pattern & Snoopy N.F.L. twin blankets available. 66" x 90. 1987. $25–30 mint in package.

Acrylic beach blanket. 45" x 72" pattern, "Tag along," packaged in reuseable plastic bag. Beach print twin blanket. 1987. $25–30 mint in package. $15–25 mint in drawstring bag.1987. Chatham.

Cotton bedspread and pillow sham, Snoopy and Belle. Sears. 1980s. Twin $40–50 set.

Peanuts Gang drapes, cotton. J.C. Penney. 1980s. $20–25 mint.

Cotton Peanut Gang sheet. J.P Stevens, Utica. 1980s. Twin sheet $10–15. Full $20–25 mint.

Peanuts Gang valance, cotton. Sears. 1980s. $5–10

Shoe bag, Snoopy and Woodstock on cloud, cotton. Cut and sew kit. F.C.I. 1980s. $10–15

Peanuts Gang curtains, cotton. Sears. Matches valance. 1980s. $15–20 mint.

Baby quilt, cotton. FCI. Made from fabric bolt. Early 1980s. $12–18 mint.

Peanuts Gang quilt and Snoopy pillow, cotton. Pillow goes in yellow pocket. Made from kit. Early 1980s. $50–75

Top for unfinished quilt, cotton. F.C.I. 1980s. $10–15

Snoopy and Woodstock baby sheet, cotton. 1970s. $10–15

Lucy pajama bag, cotton. Simon Simple. 1970s. $30–40

Plastic Snoopy on doghouse humidifier/vaporizer. Amsco Industries–Milton Bradley Co. 1970. $50–75 complete.

Pigpen, Please Clean up

Lucy, Snoopy and Charlie Brown soap from Avon. Mint condition and in the box are the only way these are valuable. 1970. $25–35

Soap dish, Snoopy's pal Woodstock. Avon. 1973. $15–25 with box.

Charlie Brown bubble bath. Snoopy liquid soap, available with blue lid also. Lucy shampoo. Milk glass with metal lid and plastic knob. Avon. Sold individually and boxed sets. Late 1960s. $15–30 each.

Charlie Brown soap dish. Avon. Mid 1970s. $15–25

Linus bath gel holder with suction cup on back. Avon. Late 1960s. $20–40 with box.

Charlie Brown non-tearing shampoo. Avon. 1969. $20–30

Snoopy and friends bath soap. Cosrich Inc. 1990. $2–4

Snoopy "Joe Soap". Grosvenor of London. 1990s. $3–5

Pig Pen Bath Foam and Charlie Brown Detangler. Snoopy Naturals, Distributed by Minnetonka. Mid 1990s. $3–5

Snoopy and friends cosmetics in carrying box. Giftique. 1990. $10–12

Snoopy nail polish and pin. Giftique. 1989. $5–8

Snoopy and Belle cologne. Creative Specialties Ltd. 1980s. $15–20 each.

Peanuts 3-pack tooth brushes. George Harrison Ltd. Early 1990s. $3–5 each.

Snoopy bubble-blowing tub. Comes with bathroom staged box and liquid bubbles. Chemtoy. Late 1970s. $25–40

Sponge bath mitts. Dragons Are Too Seldom, Inc. Early 1990s. $5–7 each.

Ceramic cup, Linus and Lucy. 4". J. Franco & Sons. 1997. $12–15. Front and back view.

Silver plate comb and brush set. Godinger. 1990s. $20–25

Cardboard boxes of Puff's tissues. Proctor and Gamble. 1988. $6–8 each.

Ceramic soap holder. Determined, 1970s. $50–60

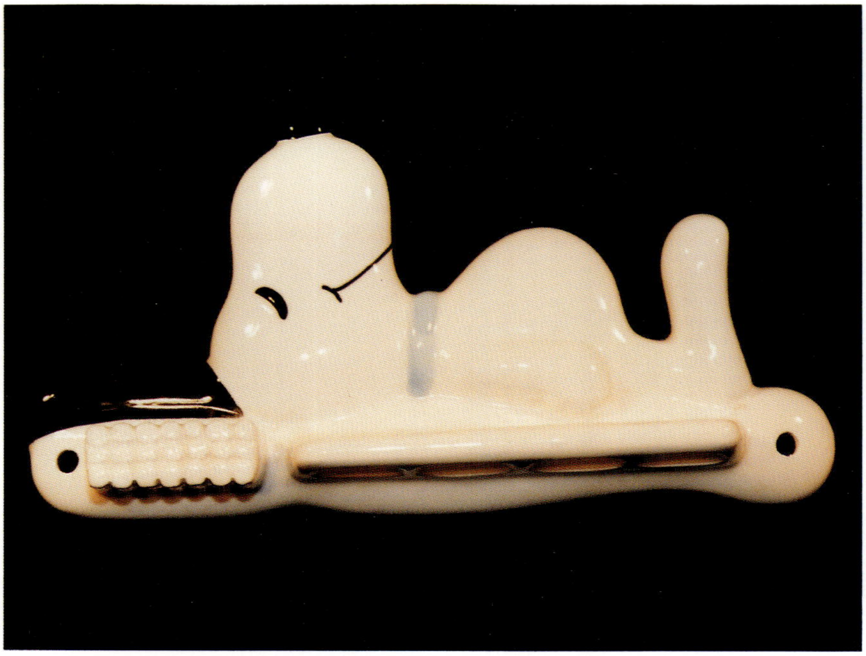

Ceramic toothbrush holder. Determined. 1979. 7 ½" x 4". $60–70

Ceramic Snoopy dish. The dish is the tub; the lid is Snoopy sitting inside bubbles with bubble on nose. 4 ½" x 3". Determined. 1979. $65–75

Ceramic Snoopy soapdish. 6 ½" x 3 ¾". Determined. 1970s. $50–60

Ceramic toothbrush holder and soap dish. Willitts. Early 1990s. $30–40 each.

Ceramic tooth brush holder, Snoopy as aviator. 7 ¾" x 5 ½" x 5". J. Franco & Sons. 1997. $15–20

Ceramic lotion pump, Snoopy. 6". J. Franco & Sons. 1997. $15–20

Ceramic lotion pump, Charlie Brown holding Woodstock. 7 ¼". J. Franco & Sons. 1997. $15–20

Ceramic soapdish, Schroeder playing piano. 7" x 3 ½" x 3 ¼". J. Franco & Sons. 1997. $15–20

Peanuts Gang Advertises to One and All

Plastic clip-ons from Butternut Bread Co. 5 to complete set. Frieda (as shown), Snoopy, Linus, Charlie Brown, Lucy. Early 1970s. $5–8 each.

Plastic clip ons from Butternut Bread. Lucy not shown. 5 to a set. $5–8 each on card.

Cardboard advertising display from Duracell batteries. 1980s. $7–10

Puzzle from Weber's Bread. Early 1970s. $30–40

Tin Snoopy button from Butternut Bread. Early 1970s. $12–15 each.

Charlie Brown poster, set of 4, cello-wrapped together. Other side reveals Snoopy as Uncle Sam. Promotional Interstate Brands. 1970s. $12–18 each. Mint set $40–60.

Pez candy display box. 1990s. $5–7

Tin can Snoopy bank from Rival. 1970s. $25–35

Dolly Madison display poster. Early 1970s. $8–12

Cardboard "Dolly Madison" lemonade stand. Came uncolored, with lemonade jug. 1980s. $45–60. Connie Porges tending the stand.

Plastic lemonade jar, goes with lemonade stand.

Dolly Madison baseball cards. 6 in set. Charlie Brown and Lucy not shown. 1983. $2–4 each.

Two-page Ford Falcon ad in full color. Peanuts characters in lower right-hand corner. 1961. $15–20

Full page Ford Falcon ad with Peanuts characters. 1962. $10–15

Environmental program from Johnnie Horizon. 1972. $25–35

Chex recipe book. Early 1990s. $3–6

Woodstock environmental poster. 1972. Johnny Horizon promotional–U.S. Dept. of Interior. $15–20

Plastic microwave dish from Chex promotion. 1990: Peanuts' 40th anniversary. $20–25

Plastic canister from Chex party mix. Promotional. 1990s. $4–6

Chex advertising tin. Mid 1990s. $5–7

Plush Snoopy advertising Northern Tissue. 1990s. $15–20

Cardboard display from NFL for Peanuts video. Display fits on top of gas pump. For three years Shell used Peanuts in their Christmas promotions. The last year it was "You're In The Super Bowl, Charlie Brown." The entire gang was featured on these posters. Shell. 1993. $7–10

Cardboard display from NFL for Peanuts video. Shell. 1993. $7–10

Cardboard display, Charlie Brown and Snoopy playing football. Shell. 1993. $7–10

Cardboard display, Lucy and Woodstock playing football. Shell. 1993. $7–10

Cardboard promotional displays, Snoopy and Peppermint Patty. Shell. Early 1990s. $7–10

Cardboard display, Charlie Brown throwing football. 1 ½ feet tall. Shell. 1993. $7–10 each.

National park poster. 1990s. $3–5

Felt pennants with sticks, Lucy and Charlie Brown. Knott's Berry Farm. 1990. Snoopy not shown. $4–6 each.

Plastic cup from A & W root beer. Early 1990s. $10–15

Plastic cup advertising Oscar Meyer. 1990s. $3–5

Camp Snoopy McDonald's baseball hat. 1983. $10–12

Meal boxes from McDonald's. Special toys for kids under 3 years old. 1990 promotion. Prices are for mint condition, in package. $4–7 mint with boxes. $3–7 each. In 1994 McDonald's featured a Happy Birthday Train–many characters were special guests. Peanuts was #12. Please note: The meal box was smaller in 1994 compared to 1990. $3–6 toy, mint in package, $3–6 for mint-condition box.

Peanuts display. McDonald's. 1993. $100–150

MetLife advertising. "A Family's Guide to Child Safety." Spanish version. 1994. $2–3

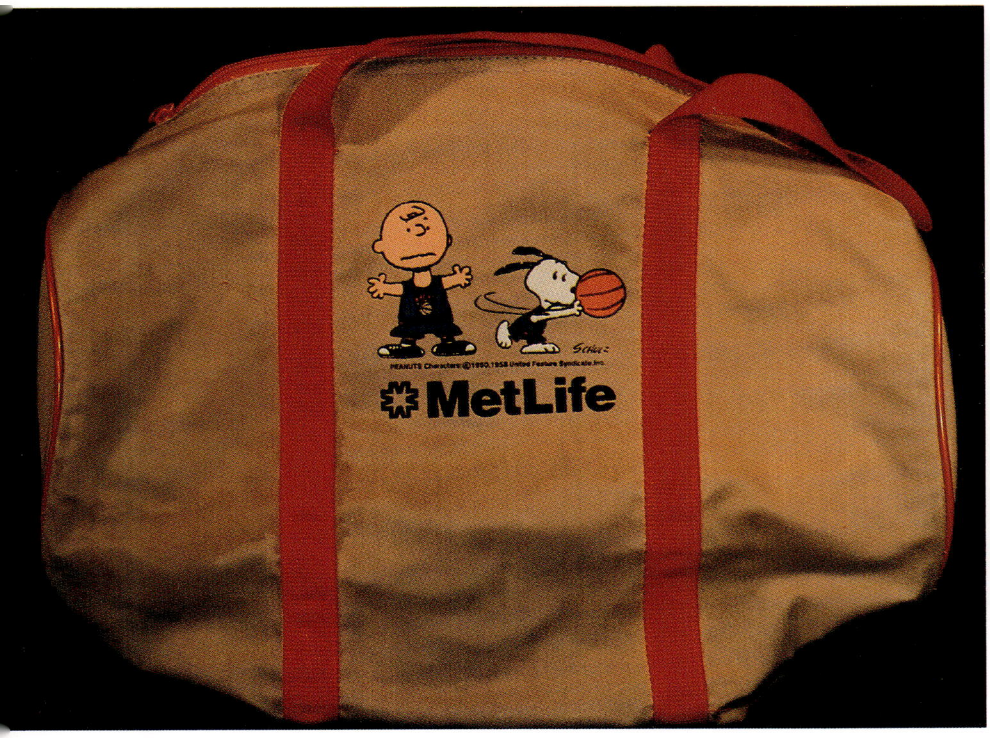

Canvas carry-all bag from MetLife. Throughout the Late 1980s–1990s MetLife sponsored many sports events with wonderful totebags. $10–15 mint.

Plastic coffee cup. MetLife. 1990s. $5–7

Advertising magnets from MetLife. 1980s–1990s. $2–3

MetLife advertising poster. Late 1980s–90s. $5–7

MetLife posters. Early 1990s. $5–7 each.

MetLife advertising poster. Late 1980s–90s. $5–7

MetLife advertising poster. Late 1980s–90s. $5–7

MetLife advertising poster. Late 1980s–90s. $5–7

MetLife advertising poster. Late 1980s–90s. $5–7

MetLife advertising poster. Mid 1990s. $5–7

Cardboard display, Snoopy. Hallmark. Mid 1980s. $10–15

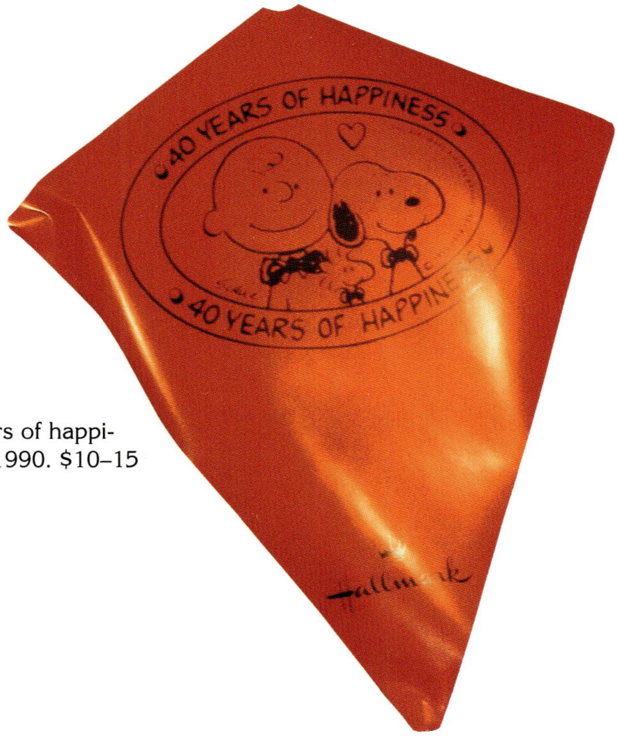

Vinyl kite commemerating 40 years of happiness. Display for Hallmark store. 1990. $10–15

Cardboard display, Peauts Gang. Hallmark. Mid 1980s. $10–15

Cardboard banner display, Woodstock, Snoopy, and Sally. Ambassador. 1990s. $15–25

Cardboard stand-up figure, "life sized", Charlie Brown. Special premium from KVC video store—buy video and send money for shipping and handling. 1990. $25–35

Cardboard Christmas display. Venture stores. 1994. 4" tall. $20–30

Cardboard display for Discover Card. Venture stores. 1994. 4 feet tall. $20–30

Nabisco special offers pamplet from box of Milk Bone dog biscuits. Mid 1990s. For a limited time Milk Bone offered good quality, unique, reasonably priced premiums by sending in money with proof of purchase from the box. $1–2 pamphlet.

Front and back view of box of Milk Bone biscuits. Nabisco. Mid 1990s. $2–4, depending on size.

What are You Wearing, Lucy?

Cotton playsuit, Peanuts Gang. 1996. Peanuts Playwear. $20–25

Cotton child's playsuit, Peanuts Gang. Peanuts Playwear. 1996. $20–25

Cotton playsuit, Charlie Brown and Snoopy. 1996. Peanuts Playwear. $20–25

Cotton playsuit, Snoopy and Sally. 1996. Peanuts Playwear. $20–25

Child's cotton sweat shirt, Peanuts Gang. 1980s. Baby Fair. Originally came with matching sweatpants. $2–5

Cotton playsuit, Peanuts Gang. 1996. Peanuts Playwear. $20–25

Cotton playsuit, Joe Cool. 1996. Peanuts Playwear. $20–25

Child's cotton tee shirt, Peanuts Gang. 1980s. $2–5

Cotton sweat shirt, Linus and Lucy with Snoopy dancing on piano. 1970s. $5–20 mint.

Child's cotton sweatshirt. Buster Brown. Late 1980s. $10–15 new.

Child's cotton jacket. Buster Brown made these for Peanuts Brand. Early 1990s. $15–20

Childs' cotton shirt, Sally. 1996. Peanuts Playwear. $12–18

Cotton sweat shirt, Charlie Brown. 1996. Peanuts Playwear. $12–18

Cotton sweat shirt, Charlie Brown. 1996. Peanuts Playwear. $12–18

Child's cotton shirt, Peanuts. 1996. Peanuts Playwear. $12–18

Child's cotton tee shirt, Linus. Buster Brown. Mid 1990s. $10–15

Child's cotton tee shirt, Peanuts Gang. Buster Brown. Mid 1990s. $10–15

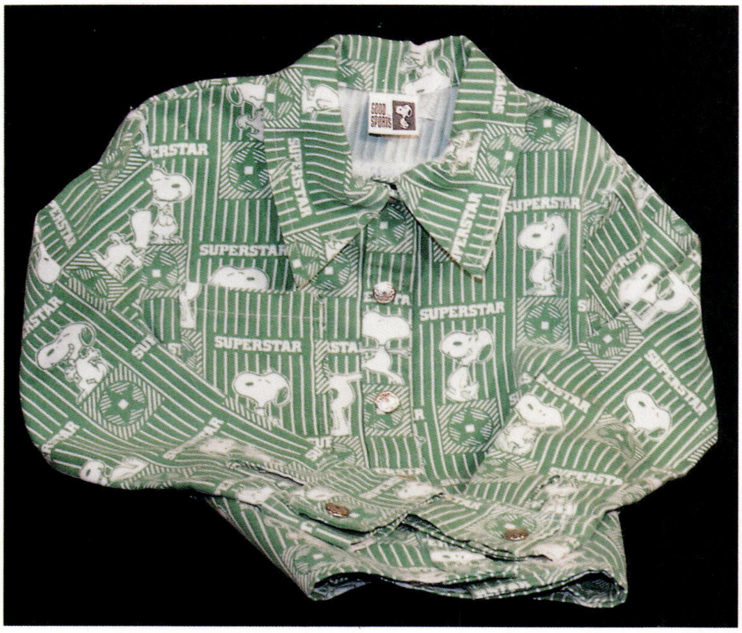

Cotton shirt, Snoopy Superstar. 1970s. $12–15

Cotton tee shirt, Earth Day. 1990. $12–15 new.

Cotton applicade sweatshirt. Licensed fabric. $10–18

Cotton sweatshirt, Peanuts Gang. Blitzz Studio. Early 1990s. $20–25

Cotton shirt with embroidered "Charlie Brown." Jostens. 1990. $30–40

Denim jacket, Camp Snoopy. 1990s. $100–125

Cotton employee's jacket, Butternut Bread. 1970s. $25–35

Cotton tee shirt, Beaglefest 4. 1995. Mall of America, Minnesota, Camp Snoopy. $6–8

Dressing our Favorite Beagle

Belle outfit. Determined. 1980s. Mint package. 10", $10–15. 15", $15–20.

Yellow Belle shirt. Came with blue jeans. Determined. 11" and 17". Late 1970s. $15–20/$20–25

Belle Christmas outfit. In the late 1970s and early 80s Determined made many outfits for various sized Snoopys, Belles and Woodstocks. Most desirable is, of course, mint in package as shown. Determined. $15–25 each.

Vinyl Belle hat box. Determined. Early 1980s. $15–20

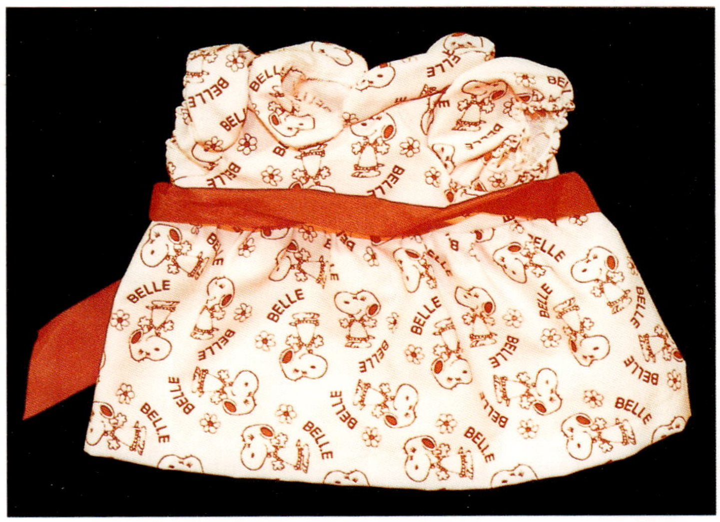

Belle's dress with Belle print. Late 1970s. Determined. 11" $15–20. 17" $20–25.

Peanuts Gang scarf. Vera. 1990s. Discontinued in 1996. $15–20

Great Accessories, Sally

Silk Christmas scarf. Vera. 1990s. Discontinued in 1996. $15–20

Peanuts Gang scarf. Vera. 1990s. Discontinued in 1996. $15–20

Cotton Peanuts handkerchief from Japan. Early 1990s. $8–12

Cotton Snoopy scarf. Vera. Early 1990s. $15–20

Silk tie, Peanuts Gang.
1990s. $20–25

Silk ties, Peanuts Gang. Mid 1990s. $20–25

Silk ties, Peanuts Gang.
1990s. $20–25

Vinyl umbrella. 1980s–90s. $7–12

Vinyl umbrella, Snoopy comic strips.
Shaw. 1980s–90s. $10–15

Vinyl umbrella, Schroeder and Lucy.
Shaw. 1980s–90s. $10–15

Vinyl belt, Peanuts Gang. 1980s. Lee. $5–7

Charlie Brown eye glass case with sunglasses, vinyl. Unknown maker and year. $5–15 case. $40–75 glasses.

Plastic Charlie Brown glasses case. Probably 1980s. $2–7, fair to mint.

Cotton bootie socks. Gold Bug. 1991. $3–5

Tin box that holds Peanuts Gang key chain. Accessories Network. Mid 1990s. $7–10

Acrylic stretch magic gloves, Lucy and Charlie Brown. Accesories Network. 1990s. $5–7

Rubber key chains, Charlie Brown and Lucy. 1990s. Accessory Network. $4–5 each.

Plastic key chain, Snoopy and Woodstock. Late 1980s–90s. Mongram Products. $4–6

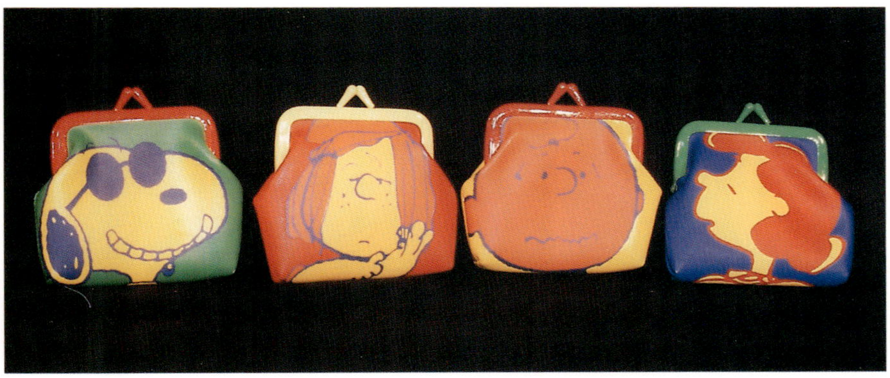

4 vinyl change purses, Peanuts Gang. Applause. Late 1980s, early 1990s. $4–6 each.

Rubber key chains, Linus and Sally. 1990s. Accessory Network. $4–5 each.

Vinyl zipper pencil case. Unknown maker. 1980s. $5–7

Cotton bag, Lucy. 1970s. Reverse side. Snoopy in booth. $18-25

Canvas bookbag, Peanuts. 1980s.
$10–15

Peanuts bookbag. Butterfly. 1980. $15–20

Mini tote bag, fabric. Butterfly. $3–5

Canvas carry-all bag, Peanuts Gang. Horizon Designs. Early 1990s. $15–20

Tote bag, Schroeder and Lucy. Horizon Designs. 1990s. $10–15

Nylon suitcase, Belle. Early 1980s. Aviva. $20–30

Plastic Peanuts organizer. 1980s. $10–15

Cotton shoe holder, Peanuts Gang. Butterfly. Early 1980s. $10–15.

Hanging shoe bag, fabric. Butterfly. 1980s. $10–15

Sewing with Marcie

Ribbon on spool. Unknown maker. Late 1980s. $15–20, mint.

Cross stitch kit, baby quilt. JCA. Inc. Early 1990s. $35–45

Hanging crib toy, cotton. Stuff and sew kit. FCI. 1980s. $8–12

Schroeder cloth patch. Determined. 1970. $7–9 in package. $4–5 loose.

Military patch. Not licensed but still collectible. 1970s. $25–35

Plastic buttons from JHB International. Early 1990s. $4–6 per card.

Embroidered cotton patches, Lucy and Linus. Probably Determined. Most likely late 1970s, early 1980s. $4–6 each.

Snoopy and Woodstock patch. 1980s. $4–6

Cloth patches, Charlie Brown and Linus. Wappan/Imported. 1980s. $4–6 in package.

Movee button. Aviva. Early 1970s. $15–20

1984 wall calendar, Snoopy. Made from fabric bolt. FCI. $6–8

Stick on, sew on vinyl patches. Peanuts Gang. Made in England. EZ International. 1980s. $3–5 each on card.

Stick on, sew on vinyl patches. Snoopy in different poses. Made in England. EZ International. 1980s. $2–3 each on card.

Peanut Gang Jewelry Store

Pin it, Lucy

Plastic pin-back buttons that flash back and forth with different pictures. Both views. $8–12 each.

Snoopy pin, Beaglefest IV. 1995. $4–6

Cloth covered pin-back buttons. Early 1980s. Butterfly. $8–12 each.

Metal fan club pins. Simon Simple. Snoopy for President—full figure, 1980. $15–20. Bicentennial button, 1976. $15–20. Plastic glitter-like button, Snoopy with stars, 1980s. $6–9. Snoopy for President with stars, Abraham and Straus promotional button. 1970s. $15–20. Snoopy for President/Webers for lunch promotional button. Early 1970s. $15–20

Peanuts Gang pin-backs. Early 1980s. Butterfly. $4–6 each.

Plastic "I'm Irish" button. Applause. 1990. $3–5

Charlie Brown Holiday Button. Hallmark. 1980s. $5–7

Linus pin. 1990s. Knott's Berry Farm. $5–7

Mini die cast pin, Snoopy on dog house and Lucy with Charlie Brown. Early 1980s. $10–15 each.

Plastic Charlie Brow
pin from Aviva.
1970s. $20–30 mi
in package.

Just Wear it, Charlie Brown

Cloisonne Schroeder earrings and pin. Aviva. 1970s. $20–25 set.

Pewter heart necklace. Starline. 1990s. $7–10

Black laquer plastic jewelry box. Glory Co. Japan. Mid 1990s. $20–25

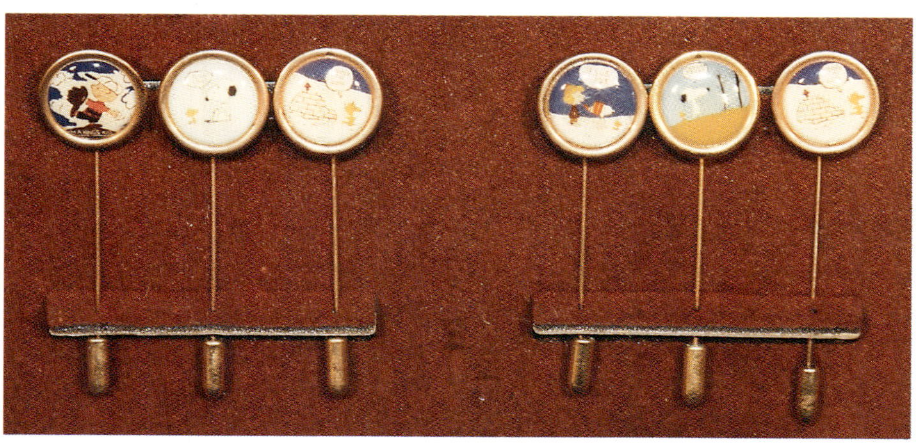

Peanuts Gang stick pins. Uncertain if licensed. Year unknown. $3–5 each.

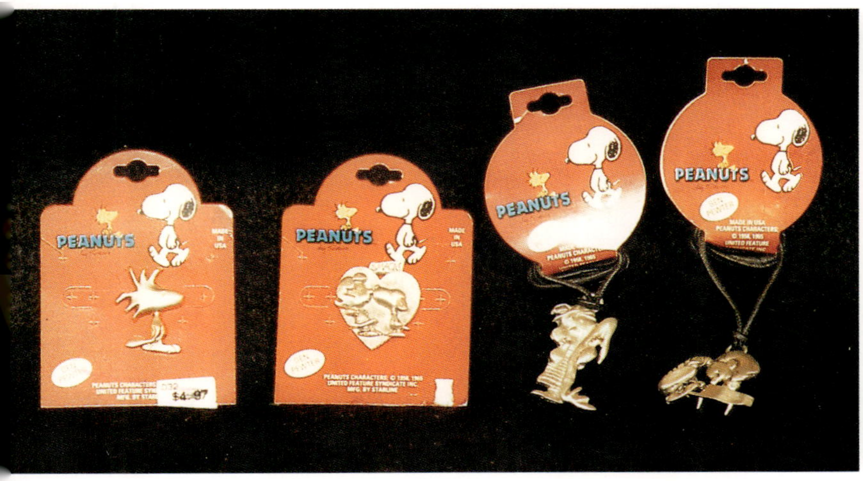

Pewter-like Peanuts Gang jewelry. Starline. Early to mid 1990s. $5–9 each.

Leather Snoopy bracelet. Probably Aviva. Fashioned like a leather keychain. 1970s. $10–12

Woodstock, Got the Time?

Plastic Snoopy watch display case. 1970s. $150–175. Timex watches, $60–80 each.

Snoopy "Hero-time" watch with patch and package. Determined. 1970s. $75–125

Snoopy watch from Armitron in original tin box. 1990s. $30–50

Snoopy Time watch. Silvertone or goldtone with various colors of watches and bands. Late 1960s. Determined. $75–100 with package.

Charlie Brown and Snoopy watch. Armitron. 1990s. $30–50

Peanuts Gang watch with plastic band. Water resistant. Japan. $60–80

Woodstock watch with leather band. Armitron. 1990s. $60–80

Snoopy watch from Armitron. As time passes the characters on TV change. Plastic. 1990s. $20–30

Schroeder musical watch from Armitron. 1990s. $60–75

Gold, Gold, Gold

Solid gold Snoopy necklace. Cartier. 1977. Chain not included. $7,000–9,000. Hard to find!

Solid gold Charlie Brown, Snoopy and Woodstock charms on gold chain. 1990s. Unknown maker. $30–50 each.

Three sets of earrings, goldtone. 1990s. $25–35 set.

Solid gold Snoopy on gold chain. 1990s. Unknown maker. Smaller 3D Snoopy, $35–45. Larger 3D Snoopy, $50–60.

Solid gold Snoopy and Woodstock charms on gold chain. Flat Snoopy gold brushed charm. 1990s. Maker unknown. $30–40. 3D Woodstock, $35–45. 3D Snoopy, $50–60.

14K gold charm bracelet and earrings. Figure of Snoopy. Each charm sold separately. Circle Fine Art Jewelry. 1996. $250–300 each charm.

Coins, Coins, Coins

Snoopy astronaut coin. Commemorates 1969 Apollo flight. Determined. $40–60

Collector's coins. Rarities, mint. Late 1980s. Issued with serial number. .999 fine silver, 1 troy oz. signed by Mintmaster, sealed in plastic coin holder in decorative cardboard booklets. $60–100 each.

Snoopy and gang collector's coins. Knott's Camp Snoopy exclusive. Coin #1 Snoopy. #2 Woodstock. #3 Linus. #4 Lucy. #5 Sally. #6 Charle Brown. Knott's Berry Farm. 1993. $20–30 set.

Woodstock, my Little Friend

Plush Reindeer Woodstock. Mechanical. Came in two other variatons: Woodstock as Santa and Woodstock plain. Plug in and head rotates. 18". Mid 1970s. $200–250

Goldwash Woodstock costume earrings and pin. 1990s. $8–12 each.

Crystal Woodstock figurine. 27MM Silver Deer Crystal. 1993. $75–125

Plush Woodstock earmuffs. Macy's. Late 1980s–90s. $12–18

Cotton Woodstock sweatshirt. Jostens Sportswear. Mid 1990s. $30–40

Cotton Woodstock sweatshirt. Jostens. Mid 1990s. $20–25

Cotton denim ladies' shirt with Woodstock on pocket. Chambrey. Early–Mid 1990s. $30–40

Ceramic Woodstock bank. Determined Productions. Mid 1970s. $15–25

Ceramic salt and pepper shakers of Woodstock holding flower. Benjamin & Medwin. Early 1990s. $15–20 set, in box.

Ceramic Woodstock on nest, ornament from general series. Determined Productions. 2 ½". 1980–81. $30–40

Ceramic cup, Woodstock on handle. 1980s. Teleflora. $10–15

Plastic bank, Woodstock on egg. 1990. Applause. $15–20

Knit cap, Woodstock. 1970s–80s. $7–10

Plastic trophy, Woodstock coming out of egg. 1970s–80s. Aviva. $8–12

Plastic trophy, Woodstock. 1970s–80s. Aviva. $8–12

Plastic trophies, Woodstock. 1970s–80s. Aviva. $8–12

Plastic trophy, Woodstock. Aviva. 1970s. $8–12

Plastic chirping Woodstock. Battery operated. Reposition tail and get different bird calls. Aviva. 1977. $15–40 with box.

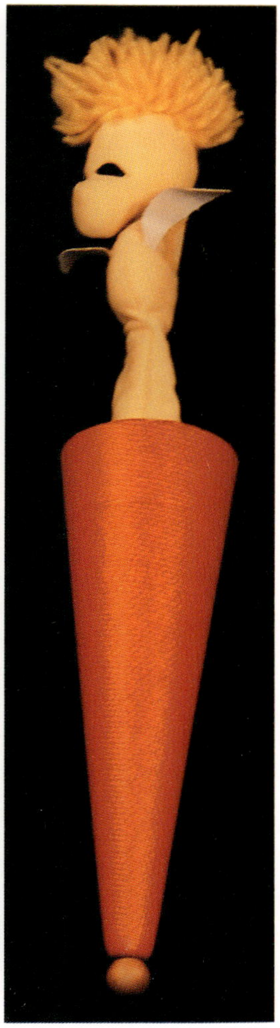

Woodstock puppet, moves up and down. Fabric Woodstock, wood stick, cardboard cone. Late 1970s–80s. Aviva. $25–35

Plastic toy, Woodstock driving ice cream truck. Aviva. Late 1970s–early 1980s. $8–12

Plastic wind-up walking Woodstocks. Aviva. 1970s. Wind him up and he hops. $5–8 each in package.

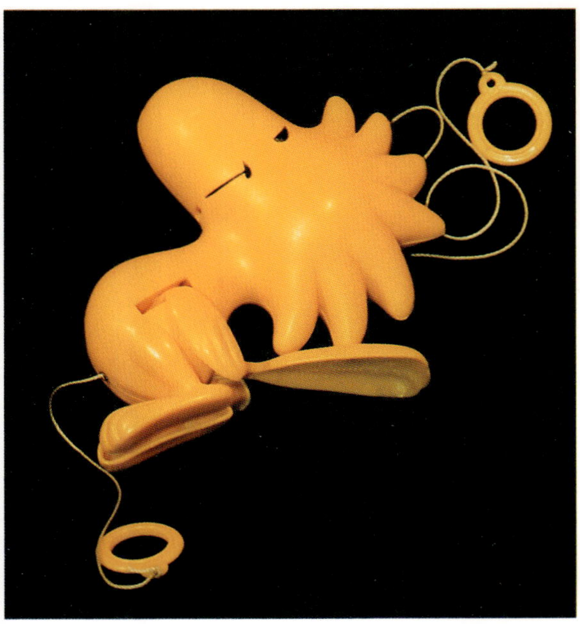

Plastic Woodstock. Pull the string and he climbs up and down the rope. Aviva. Late 1970s. $30–40 with box.

Plastic Woodstock free wheeling toy. Aviva. Early 1980s. $6–10

Plastic Woodstock on nest. Motorized toy. Aviva. Late 1970s. $15–25, with box.

Plastic Woodstock walker. Wind him up and he hops. Aviva. Mid 1970s. $5–8 in package.

Plastic Woodstock on bikes. Late 1980s–90s. ITT. $7–12 each, in package.

Woodstock driving ice cream truck. Aviva. 1970s. $8–12 in package.

PVC Woodstock coming out of egg. Fun figure from Whitmans. Mid 1990s. $2–4

Velour Woodstock toy. Filled with sawdust. Determined. 1970s. $10–15

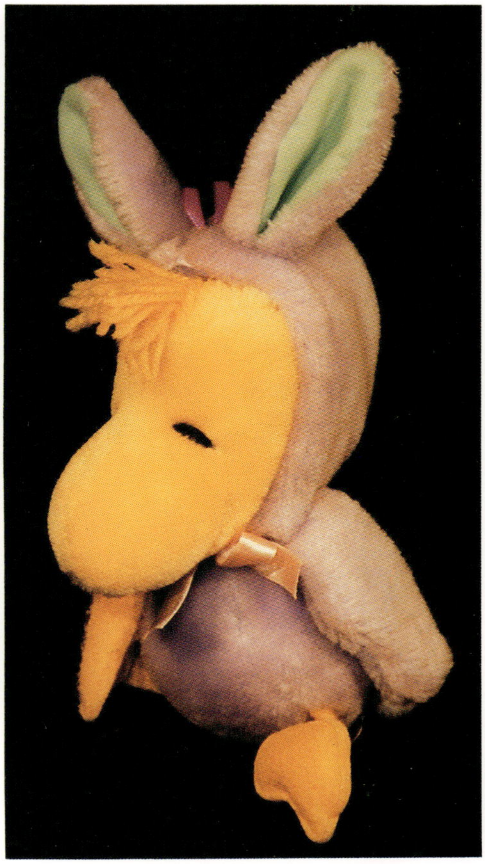

Plush toy, Woodstock dressed as bunny. He chirps. Applause. 1990. $15–20

Beanbag-like plush Woodstock. Filled with crushed nutshells. Butterfly. 1980. $12–20 mint.

Plush Woodstock. He chirps. Determined. 1980s. $15–20

Plush Woodstock in Scout outfit. Early 1980s. Determined. $20–30

Plush toy, Woodstock with bunny ears. He chirps. Easter Beagle's Best Friend. Applause. 1990. $15– 20

Plush Woodstock. Applause. 1990. $5–10

Plush Woodstock, Santa's helper. Applause. Early 1990s. $25–35

Plastic Woodstock keychain. 1980s. Japan. $4–6

Plastic Woodstock sun catcher. Snoopy Sunshiner. Aviva. Late 1970s. $15–20

Rubber dog toy, Woodstock laying down. Con Agra Pet Products. 1980s–90s. $4–6

Vinyl squeak toy, Santa Woodstock. Con Agra Pet Products. 1980/90s. $4–6

Resin Gold Medal Friend Award. Willits. 1990s. $20–25

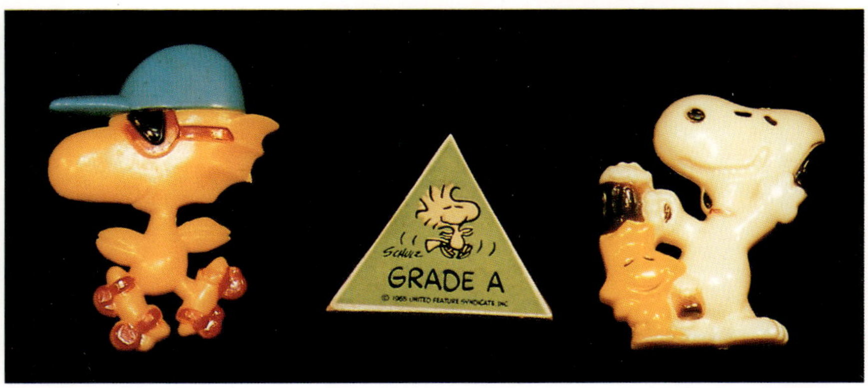

Plastic magnets, Snoopy and Woodstock. 1980s. Triangle is a sticker mounted on wood and made into a magnet. $1–4 each in package.

Over there, (Foreign)

Oh, What Beautiful Music, Schroeder

Ceramic music box. Plays "Beautiful Dreamer". Sekiguchi Co. Ltd. Japan. 1997. $40–50

Ceramic music box. Plays "How much is that doggie in the window?" Sekiguchi Co. Ltd. Japan. 1997. $40–50

Ceramic music box. Sekiguchi Co. Ltd. Japan. 1997. $40–50

Ceramic music box. Plays "Do–Re–Me".Sekiguchi Co. Ltd. Japan. 1997. $40–50

Ceramic music box. Plays "The Entertainer". Sekiguchi Co. Ltd. Japan. 1997. $40–50

Light up my World with Fine Ceramics

Ceramic Japanese nodders. 1990s. $60–75 each or $500 set.

Plastic lighted revolving globe. Glory Co. Ltd. Japan. 1990. $150–225

Ceramic Peanut Gang banks. Japan. 1990s. $30–50 each.

Peanuts' 45th Anniversary plate, ceramic. 1995. Japan. $60–75 each.

Ceramic heart-shaped planter. Determined. Mid 1970s. 4". $20–30

Peanuts' 45th Anniversary plate, ceramic. 1995. Japan. $60–75 each.

Peanuts' 45th Anniversary plate, ceramic. 1995. Japan. $60–75 each.

Peanuts' 45th Anniversary plate, ceramic. 1995. Japan. $60–75 each.

Ceramic picture frame. 6 ½" x 4 ¾". Denz. Japan. Mid 1990s. $45–55

Plastic super lunch rice bowl with chopsticks. 1990s. Japan. $20–25

Ceramic rice dish with chopsticks. Determined Productions. Japan. 1990s. $18–25

Glass is Clearly Fine

Fluted textured dish with box. Determined Productions. Japan. 7" x 4". Late 1980s. $20–25

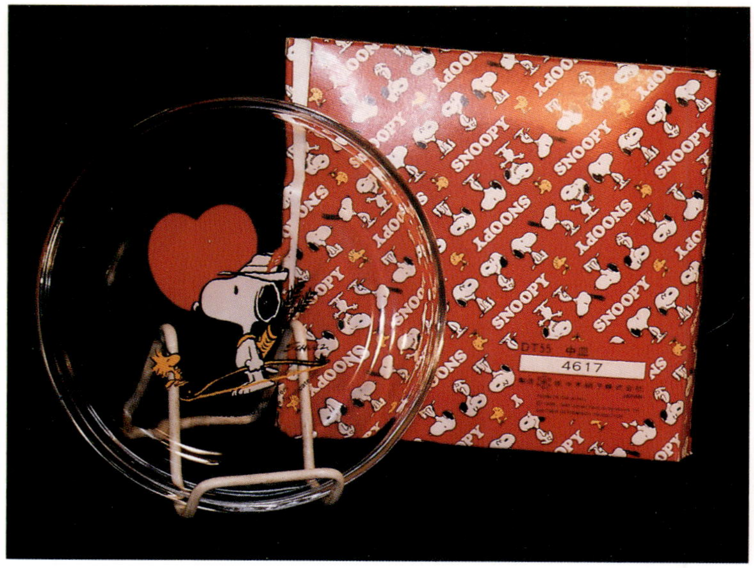

Dish with box. Determined. Japan. Late 1980s. $20–25

Dish with box. Determined. Japan. Late 1980s. $20–25

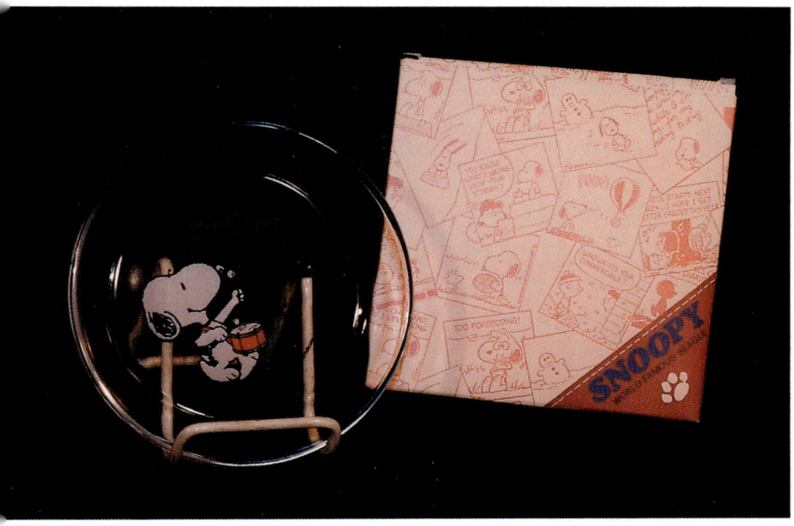

Fluted dish with box. Determined. Japan. Late 1980s. $20–25

Glass bud vase. Determined Productions. Japan. Late 1980s. 8" high. $20–25

Heart-shaped dish with box. Determined. Japan. Late 1980s. $15–20

Glass cookie jar with box. Determined. Japan. Late 1980s. $20–25

Glass star-shaped dish with box. Determined productions. Japan. Late 1980s. $20–25

Glass boot with box. Determined. Japan. Late 1980s. $13–17

Glass boots, Snoopy and brothers with Woodstock. Japan. 1990s. $20–25 set.

Vase with box. Determined. Japan. Late 1980s. $15–20

Glass goodie jar with box. Determined. Japan. Late 1980s. $15–20

Glass vase with box. Determined productions. Japan. Late 1980s. 6" high. $25–35

Peanuts Gang glasses with gold trim. Sasaki Glass Co. Ltd. 1990s. $50–60 set.

Glass set. Front and back view. 1990s. Japan. What? Sleep, Smile, Laugh, Look. $25–30

Snoopy glasses. Japan. 1990s. $30–40

Cups, Cups, Cups

Ceramic Sally cups. Japan. 1990s. $20–25 set.

Plastic cup, "Everyone's favorite beagle since 1950." Japan. 1990s. $7–10

Ceramic cup. Determined Productions. Japan. 1990s. $15–20

Ceramic Snoopy cup. Japan. 1990s. $15–20

Ceramic Snoopy cup. Japan. 1990s. $10–12

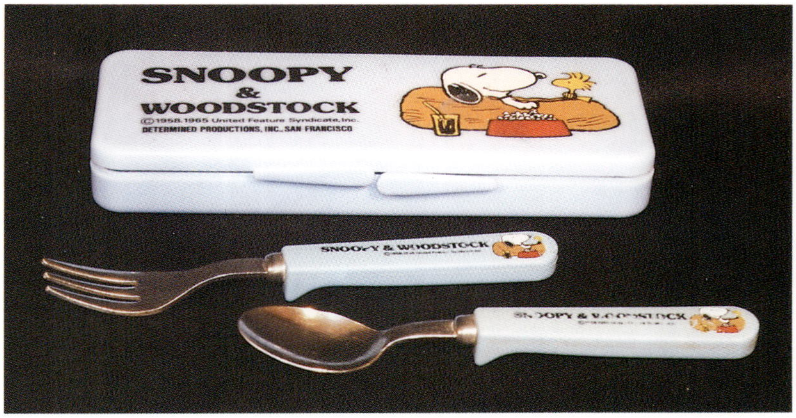

Silverware set. Determined Productions. Japan. 1980s. $9–12

Silverware. Determined Productions. Japan. 1990s. $3–4 each.

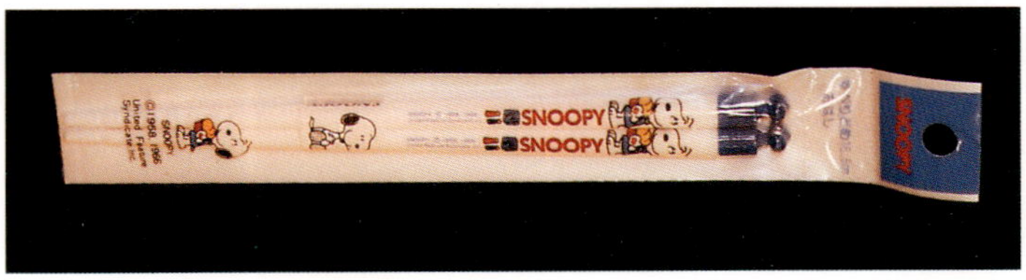

Plastic chopsticks. Hallmark. Japan. 1990s. $6–8

Package of tissues, premium from Sanwa Bank. Japan. $3–5

Snoopy and his friends facial tissue. Personal pack. Japan. $3–5

Royale 2-ply tissue. England. Unknown year. $3–5

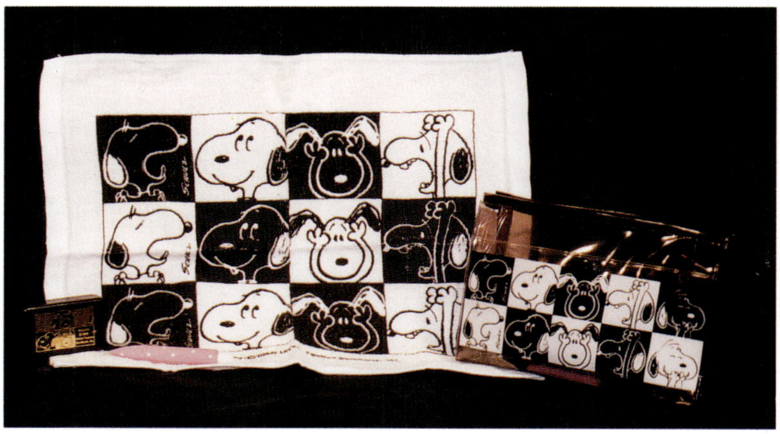

Toiletry set. Toothbrush and paste, wash cloth, soap. Determined Productions. Sanrio. Japan. 1990s. $15–20

Wet Wipes. 7" tall. Determined Productions. Japan. 1990s. $7–10

Stationary Time

Peanuts stamp set. Butterfly. Japan. 1990s. $7–10

Peanuts school life bulletin board with eraser, chalk, magnets, scribble board. Butterfly. Japan. 1980s. $20–25

Daily planning set. Germany. Done by Graphicia Creative. Printed by Giovanni Trimboli. Late 1980s. $20–25 set.

Note pads. Japan. 1990s. 1" x 2". $2–4 each.

Snoopy plastic rubber stamper and holder. Butterfly. Japan. $4–6 each.

Snoopy and Charlie Brown diary. Japan. 1990s. $12–15

Snoopy pencil sharpener, Woodstock eraser. 1980s–1990s. Japan. $4–6 each.

Lucy matches. Japan. 1980s–90s. $3–4

Peanuts Gang on cover of address book. 1990s. Japan. $12–15

Snoopy baby album. Hallmark. Japan. Kokuyo. Mid 1990s. 14" x 14". $35–45

Snoopy photo albums, Japan. 1980s–1990s. $15–25 each.

Kuwait coloring books. 1990s. $10–15 each.

Read a Book, Charlie Brown

Storybook, *Vas–y, Charlie Brown*. French version of *You Can Do It, Charlie Brown*. Holt, Rinehart and Winston. Paperback. 1969. $15–20 because it is French.

Spanish comic book. Price depends on condition. $10–30

Peanuts book, French. Holt, Rinehart & Winston. $10–20

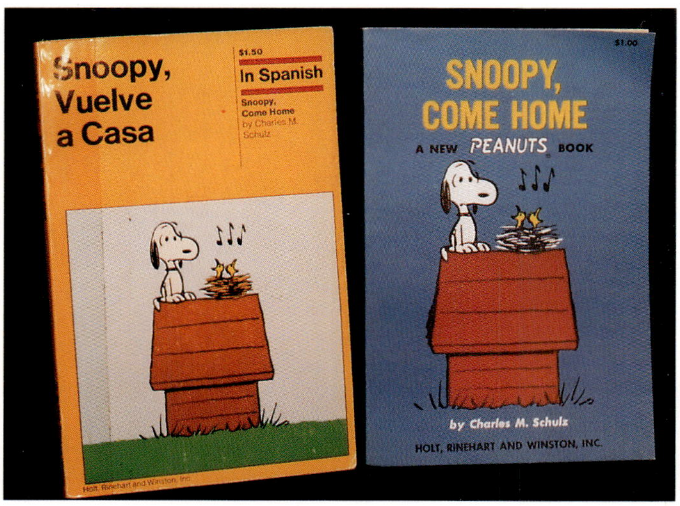

Snoopy book, both Spanish and American versions. Holt, Rinehart & Winston Inc. $10–20

Charlie Brown book, both Spanish and American versions. Holt, Rinehart & Winston. $10–20 each.

Send Me a Postcard, Peppermint Patty

Sticker postcards from Italy. 1980s. $6–8 each.

Sticker postcards from Portugal. 1980s. $6–8 each.

Sticker postcards from Italy. 1980s. $6–8 each.

Postcards from Finland. 1980s. $4–6 each.

Sticker postcards from Italy. 1980s. $6–8 each.

Postcards from Finland. 1980s. $4–6 each.

Sticker postcards from Portugal. 1980s. $6–8 each.

Postcards from Finland. 1980s. $4–6 each.

Postcards from Japan. 1980s. $4–6 each.

Postcards from Japan. 1980s. $4–6 each.

Postcards from Italy. 1980s. $4–6 each.

Postcards from Germany. 1980s. $4–6 each.

Marcie, Hand Me that Tin

Tin food containers. Daiwa, Japan. 1990s. $8–12 each.

Snoopy sewing set in tin box. Peanuts Gang. Japan. 1990s. $20–25

Tin box. Creart, Japan. 1980s–90s. $15–20

Mini metal lunch pail. Determined Productions.6" x 6 ½" x 2 ½". 1990s. $12–18

Metal lunch pail. Determined Productions. 8" x 5" x 5". 1990s. Japan. $20–25

Metal pencil case with tray. Barunson Fancy Co. Ltd. Made in Korea. 1990s. $12–16

Hang it Up, Lucy

Peanuts pins.The history of Peanuts 1950–1995. Back in 1950 when Charles Schulz first introduced Charlie Brown to the "funny pages" across America, few people realized the impact this character (and the 15 others which followed) would have world wide. Signature Authentics was granted a license for an exclusive pin set to depict these Peanut characters in chronological order showing the year of introduction to the comic strip. From Charlie Brown in 1950 to Eudora in 1978, each character has his or her own stunning full-color pin of exceptional quality. These 16 pins have been mounted on acid-free matte board and meticulously framed in rich cherry wood with gold inlay and protective glass to preserve the value of these pins for eternity. A brass center plate and titles beneath each figure printed in gold ink narrate the history.1996. $125–150

Poster from Japan. The Daisy Hill puppies. 1995. $5–8

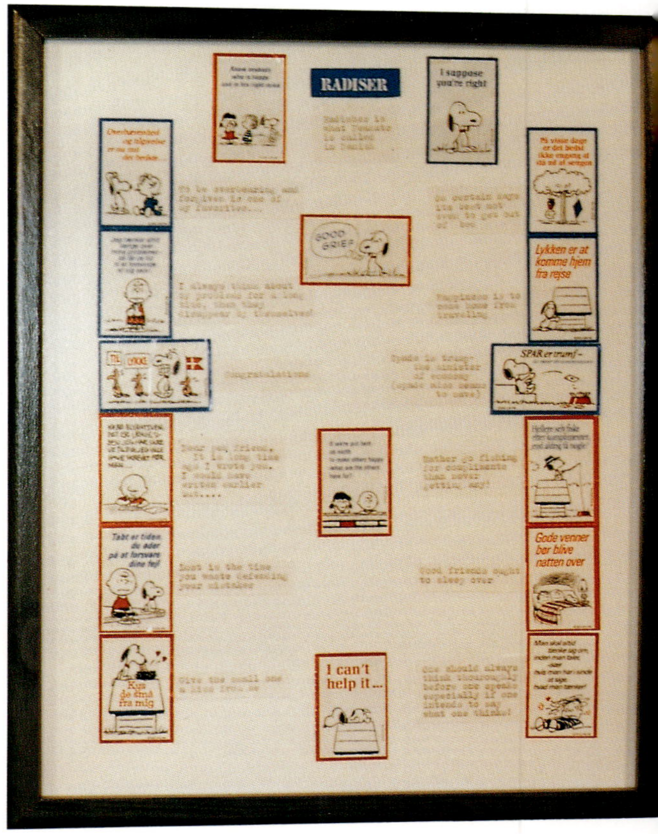

These Danish stickers came in booklet. Lick them and stick them. "Radiser" in Danish means Snoopy. Early 1990s. Framed with translations. $20–25

Dry it up, Pigpen

Japanese handkerchief. Hallmark. 1980s–90s. $7–10

Left and below: Terry cloth Snoopy and friends rug runner. Japan. 1990s. $100–125

Cotton washcloth. Japan. 1990s. $7–12.

England linen towel. Late 1980s. $25–30

Flying Ace terry washcloth. Blackstaff Textiles Ltd. Ireland. 1980s–90s. $5–8

Terry bath towel and wash cloth. Blackstaff Textiles Ltd. Ireland. 1980s–90s. $20–30 set.

Snoopy terry washcloth. Blackstaff Textiles Ltd. Ireland. 1980s–90s. $5–8

Snoopy terry washcloth. Blackstaff Textiles Ltd. Ireland. 1980s–90s. $5–8

Terry bath towel. Blackstaff Textiles Ltd. Ireland. 1980s–90s. $15–20

Bag it, Sally

Charlie Brown bag. Japan. Nylon. Phoenix Crp. Ltd. Distributed by Kutsuwa. 1990s. $15–20

Peanuts Gang cloth bag. Determined Productions. Japan. 1990s. $10–15

Snoopy handbag. Japan. Matsumoto. Early 1990s. $15–20

Fabric snack bag. Japan. 1980s/90s. $9–12

Large totebag. Determined Productions. Sanrio. Japan. 1990s. $20–25

Cotton Lucy and Sally tote bag. Familiar. 1990s. Japan. $7–10

Peanuts Gang cloth bag. Determined Productions. Made for Familiar. Japan. 1990s. $10–15

Snoopy fanny pack. Determined productions. Japan. 1990s. $16–20

Die cast metal miniature CB toys from ESCI. Italy. 1980s. $40–60 each.

Plastic McDonald's toys from Japan. 1990s. In Japan, toys are not placed in meals—they are sold separately. $7–9 each.

Canadian McDonald's Premiums. 1990s. $5 each in package. $20–30 set in package.

Cotton stuffed Mexican Snoopy, learning toy. Not mint. Desirable because of uniqueness. Determined. Late 1980s–90s. $20–25

Cotton child's tee shirt. Familiar Snoopy. Japan. $10–15

Plastic mirror. Japan. 1990s. $10–15

Cotton stuffed Snoopy learning toy. Determined. Late 1980s–90s. $20–25

Let's Eat, Snoopy

Peanuts Gang cereal boxes from Japan. 1994. $5–8

Snoopy Cola can. A.G. Barr & Co. Ltd. England. 1980s. $20–25

Peanuts Gang cereal boxes from Japan. 1994. $5–8

Pepsi soda pop tops with the Peanuts Gang on top. Mexico. 1980s. $2–3 each.

Snoopy Fruiti's candy tin. Holland. 1980s. $20–30

Snoopy, Snoopy, how does your garden grow?

Ceramic Snoopy on doghouse planters. 7 ¾". $60–70. 6 ¼". $50–60. 4 ¾". $40–50

Ceramic Snoopy on doghouse planter. 7 ¾". Unkown maker, probably Determined. 1970s. $60–70

Ceramic block-shaped planters A to E. 3" sq. Determined. Mid 1970s. $35–45

Ceramic shoe-shaped planters. Pink or blue laces. 3 ½". Determined. 1970s. $50–60

Ceramic star-shaped Snoopy planter. 4 ¼". Determined. Mid 1970s. $40–50

Ceramic planters. Determined. Mid 1970s. Cradle, 2 ½" x 3" x 3 ½". $45–55 Cup, 2 ½" x 2 3/8". $30–40

Ceramic purse-shaped planter. 4 ¾". Determined. Mid 1970s. $60–75

Ceramic square planter. 3 ½" x 4 ¼". Determined. Mid 1970s. $60–75

Ceramic Snoopy rainbow planter. Determined. Mid 1970s. 5 ½" x 4 ¼". $35–40

Ceramic Snoopy planter. 7". Determined. Mid 1970s. $65–75

Ceramic planter, Snoopy as Vaudeville performer. 4 ¼". Determined. Mid 1970s. $60–75

Ceramic star heart-shaped planter. 3 ¼". Determined. Mid 1970s. $45–55

Ceramic Snoopy planter. 3 ½" x 4 ¾". Determined. Mid 1970s. $45–55

Ceramic Snoopy heart-shaped rose holder. Determined. Mid 1970s. 3 ¾" x 4 ½". $35–40

Ceramic square planter. Strawberry on one side, pineapple, watermelon, banana. Determined. Mid 1970s. 3" x 3". $45–55

Ceramic Snoopy on heart planter. 4". Determined. Mid 1970s. $45–50

Ceramic planter, full figure Snoopy next to small barrel. 4 ¼". Determined. Mid 1970s. $60–75

Ceramic planter, smiling Snoopy sitting in front of red heart. Determined. Mid 1970s. 5". $55–65

Ceramic Snoopy with barrel planter. 6 ¾". Determined. Mid 1970s. $75–100

Ceramic planter, Snoopy and Woodstock sitting near tree stump. 4 ¼" x 3". Determined. Mid 1970s. $35–45

Ceramic mailbox planter. 3 ¼". Determined. Mid 1970s. $45–55

Ceramic Snoopy planter. Determined. 1970s. $30– 40

Ceramic planter, Snoopy on basket. 5 ¾". Determined. Mid 1970s. $40–50

Ceramic planter, Snoopy and Woodstock near doghouse. 5" x 5". Determined. Mid 1970s. $60–70

Ceramic bowl planter. 2 ½" x 4 ½". Determined. Mid 1970s. $40–50

Ceramic planter, Woodstock with basket. 4 ½" x2 ½" x 4". Determined. Mid 1970s. $45–55. Not shown: Snoopy leaning against basket, same size. $45–55

Ceramic planter, Snoopy hanging on bowl. 4 ¼". Determined. Mid 1970s. $75–85. Not shown: Same but smaller size, 3", $75–85

Ceramic book-shaped planter. 3 ½" x 5". Determined. Mid 1970s. $35–45

Ceramic octagon planter. Determined. Mid 1970s. 2 ½" x 4 ½". $30–40

Ceramic kidney-shaped planter. 2". Determined. Mid 1970s. $35–45

Ceramic planters. Left to right. 3 ¼", $35–40. 2 ½", $30–40. 2", $20–30. Determined. 1970s.

Ceramic bucket-shaped planter. Metal handle missing. 4 ¾". $45–50

Ceramic sitting Snoopy planter. Determined. Mid 1970s. 5". $45–50

Ceramic cup and saucer planter. 3" x 4". Determined. Mid 1970s. $50–60

Ceramic pot planter. Determined. Mid 1970s. 3 ¼". $35–45

Ceramic watering can-shaped planter. Holds 3 tools. 3". Determined. Mid 1970s. $40–50

Ceramic watering can planter. 4¾". Determined. Mid 1970s. $45–55

Ceramic pitcher-shaped planter. Determined. Mid 1970s. 4 ½". $40–50

Ceramic cowboy boot planter. 4 ¾". Determined. 1980. $45–55

Plush Snoopy attached to plastic doghouse. Flowers were inside doghouse. 10". Early 1990s. Teleflora. $20–30

Wooden Snoopy and Woodstock yard ornament. Avon. Early 1990s. $20–25

Ceramic vases. Determined. Mid 1970s. $45–60 each.

Ceramic vase. 5 ½" x 2 ½". Front and back view. Determined. Mid 1970s. $50–60

Ceramic vases. 5 ½". Determined. Mid 1970s. $45–60 each. Reverse on left "Love is walking hand in hand". Reverse on right "To the bunny slope".

Ceramic vase, Snoopy and Woodstock. Two sizes: 8" x 5" and 1 ½" x 3 ¼". Denz. Japan. Mid 1990s. $70–80

Glass flower vase. 6". Early 1990s. Japan. $15–20

Ceramic toothpick holders. Determined. Mid 1970s. 2"–2 ½". $20–30 each.

Ceramic bowl. 5" x 4". Determined, 1970s. $35–40

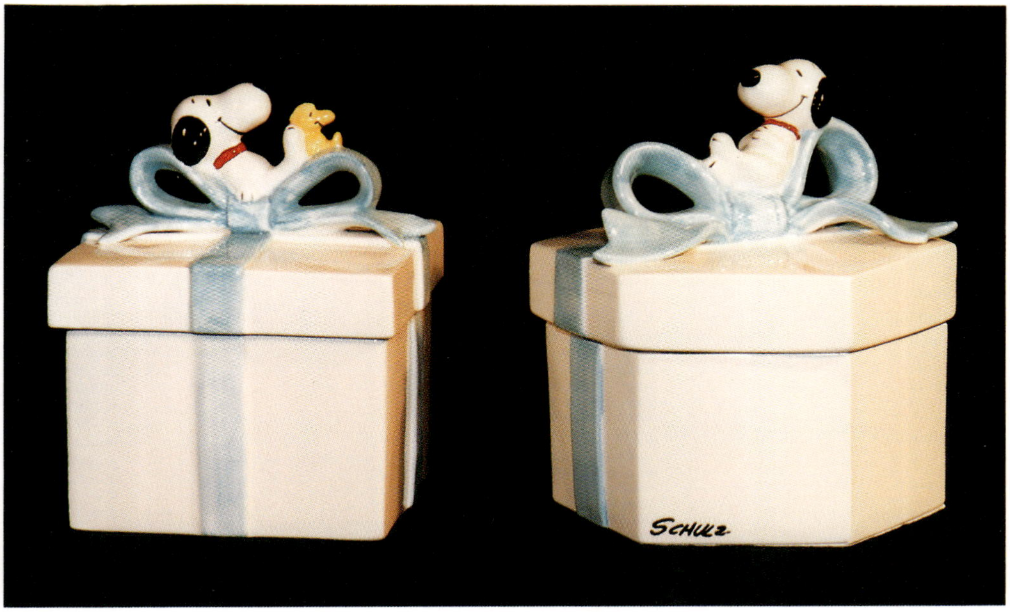

Gift boxes. Left. 3" square. Right 4 ½" x 3 ½". Determined. Early 1970s. $90–120 each.

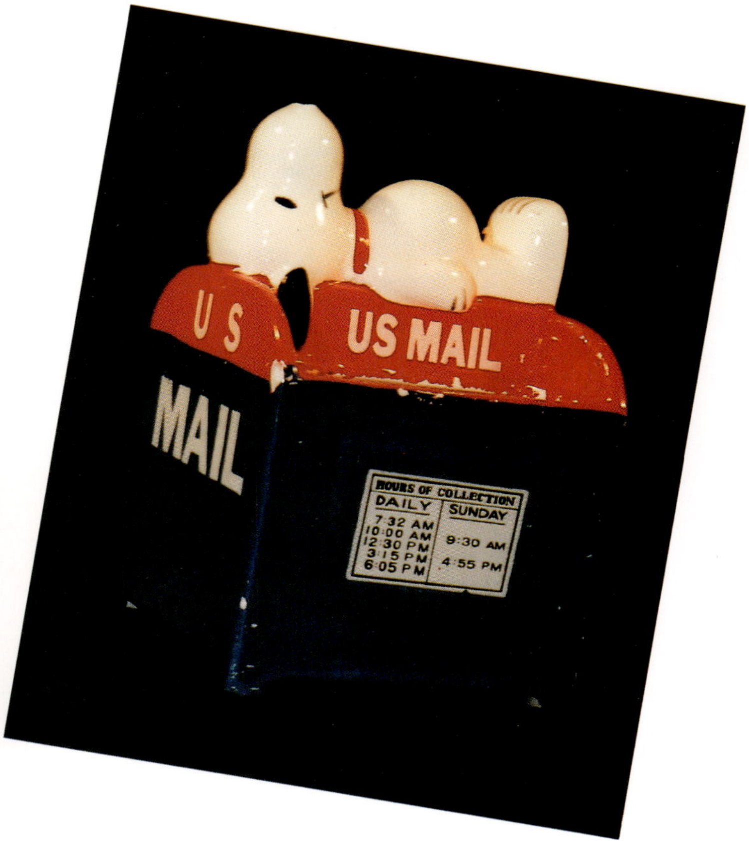

Ceramic Snoopy on mailbox. Determined. Mid 1990s. 3 ½". $35–45

Ceramic Snoopy with red heart pen holder. 3". Butterfly. Mid 1970s. $30–40

Go Fly a Kite, Robert Meyer

As as collector, one never knows when or how chance will smile at you. On a chance meeting of Robert Meyer we began to converse only to find out he was an artist who drew, of all things, Snoopy. He said he designed Snoopy kites for Determined Productions while working with a company called Crumdum Manufacturing in St. Louis, Missouri, makers of Top Flight Kites. He told me he still had several kites and some original artwork from his designs, and offered to send them to me. I told him I would love that—secretly believing he would forget or have a change of heart. What a surprise to me when the next day a package was delivered to my work with these treasures inside. A special thank you to Robert Meyer for his graciousness.

Original kite art by Robert Meyer. $20–25

Advertising pamphlet for Top Flight Kites. $5–10

Advertising picture of promotional display. $5–10. Actual display with kites. $75–100

Production cell for *Photographing Advertising* pamphlet. Hand-painted background. Cell only, $100–150. Triple matted and framed, $250–350.

Production cell for *Photographing Advertising* pamphlet. Hand-painted background. Cell only, $100–150. Triple matted and framed, $250–350.

SNOOPY
goes to the
WHITE HOUSE

The Easter Egg Roll is the longest-running traditional happening at the White House, and this year Crunden Martin's SNOOPY kites became part of that tradition. It was a surprised Crunden Martin telephone operator who heard, "This is the White House calling - let me talk to someone about kites!" We produced the official White House SNOOPY kites and presented a full display of SNOOPY and other Top Flite kites for the occasion. There was lots of Easter Egg Rolling and Kite Flying - everybody had a ball!

CRUNDEN CM MARTIN
MANUFACTURING COMPANY ST. LOUIS, MO.

Snoopy Goes to the White House, advertising. Easter 1982. $5–10

Kite with package. $5–20 mint, with package.

Kite with package. $5–20 mint with package.

Bibliography

Boomer magazine, Jim Fanning, April, 1995. Dubuque: Antique Trader Publicatons.

Johnson, Rheta Grinslay. *"Good Grief." The story of Charles Schulz*. New York: Pharos Book, 1989.

Gertler, Nat. "How the Cast Evolved from the Generic to the Special." *Comic Buyer Guide,* #1254: November 28, 1997. Kraus Publications.

Holt, Charles M. *You Don't Look 35, Charlie Brown*. New York: Holt, Rhinehart, Winston, 1985.

Schulz, Charles M. *Peanuts Jubilee: My Life & Art with Charlie Brown & Others*. New York: Holt, Rinehart, & Winston, 1975.